WILLIAM WORDSWORTH
AND
ANNETTE VALLON

PRESUMED MINIATURE PORTRAIT OF
ANNETTE VALLON

ÉMILE LEGOUIS

WILLIAM
WORDSWORTH

AND

ANNETTE VALLON

1922
LONDON & TORONTO
J. M. DENT & SONS LTD.
NEW YORK: E. P. DUTTON & CO.

CONTENTS

v

LIST OF ILLUSTRATIONS

PREFACE

SOME time after I had published *The Early Life of William Wordsworth*, in the last years of the last century, I met in London my friend Thomas Hutchinson, now deceased, who was soon after to make himself known as the erudite editor of Wordsworth, Shelley and Lamb. He had many times encouraged and helped me with his advice while I was preparing my book. In the course of our talk he asked me whether I was aware of a well-established tradition in the Coleridge family that William Wordsworth, during his stay in France, had of a young French lady a *son*, who afterwards visited him at Rydal Mount. This statement which mixed truth with some error—an error which can now be easily accounted for—made me regret that I had not known the fact beforehand, so as to alter some pages of my work which were flatly contradicted by it. But as I had then turned to other subjects, I let the thing pass without more comment, and allowed the story to sleep for many years, not hiding it from those who were concerned with the poet's life but never committing it to print.

Then came the time when Professor George Harper of Princeton University began to write his masterly biography of the poet. I told him the little I knew, but no further progress was made till he discovered among the British Museum manuscripts a series of letters written by the poet's sister, Dorothy Wordsworth, to Mrs. Clarkson, the wife of the anti-slavery apostle, wherein clear mention was made of a French lady named Madame Vallon (Annette) and of a daughter of hers named Caroline whom Dorothy called her niece. Their Paris address was also given in the same letters.

Once furnished with this clue, Professor Harper could give us a first sketch of the love-story in his *William Wordsworth, His Life, Works and Influence*, which came out in 1916. Having soon after come to France again during the war to help in the American Hospital of Neuilly, he devoted his very scanty leisure to further research and was so fortunate as to find out some documents of great importance, such as the birth and marriage certificates of Caroline Wordsworth. He, moreover, identified Annette as the sister-in-law of a Madame Vallon whose memoirs of the revolutionary times had appeared in 1913.

All these discoveries he generously imparted to me while he was in Paris, but I must confess that though they strongly impressed me on the spot, the terrible circumstances—the war was then at its darkest hour —soon drove the precise facts from my mind, leaving only the remembrance of their general interest. When Professor Harper had to return to his university, unwilling to leave his research only half done, he challenged me to bring it to an end. But I had no such design at the time, and might never have turned to the task at all, had not the English publisher of my book on *The Early Life of Wordsworth* told me last year of his intention to issue a second edition of that work. I answered that I owed it to the reader not to publish again without making the corrections and additions necessitated by later discoveries. I therefore set out to write an appendix on the relations between Wordsworth and Annette. For this I began to dip into our Records, national and local, those of Paris, Orleans and Blois. Besides the documents formerly revealed to me by Professor Harper and quite recently published by him at the Princeton University Press under the title of *Wordsworth's French Daughter*, I lighted on many others which he had not the time to hunt for, and, by degrees, the French family of the Vallons assumed a definite shape before my eyes. It was my good fortune to get into touch at last with some living members of that family, the descendants of Wordsworth and Annette on one side, and of Annette's brother Paul on the other. The result of my researches appeared in the *Revue des Deux Mondes* of the 1st April and 1st May 1922, but the exigencies of the Review precluded all recognition of my debt to those who had done most to help in the completion of my labour.

First of all, I beg respectfully to thank Madame René Blanchet, the eldest grandchild of Madame Vauchelet, who was herself the poet's eldest grand-daughter. To her I owe, among other valuable information, the curious copies of Caroline's marriage contract and of the petition to the king made on behalf of Annette by her aristocratic friends in 1816; also the fine portrait of the poet's daughter Caroline in her old age, and the essay on Words-worth's poetry written for the special benefit of Caroline's third daughter, Madame Marquet.

I am also exceedingly grateful to Madame Lecoq-Vallon, the descendant of Annette's brother Paul

Vallon, who had already made extensive private
inquiries into the family's early history and treasured-
up recollections of the revolutionary times. By her
or through her I was informed of many circumstances
relating to Paul Vallon. She also communicated to
me the interesting researches of Abbé Gallerand, the
Director of Blois Seminary, on Paul and Annette's
uncles, the priests Charles Olivier and Claude Vallon.
But she did more than all by letting me know that
a double letter of Annette to William and Dorothy
Wordsworth, written in 1792, had quite recently been
discovered in the Records of Blois by the learned
Archivist of that town, M. Guy Trouillard. I owe
her much besides for the establishment of the Vallon
genealogy. To her father, M. Omer Vallon, I am
indebted for the right of reproducing the presumed
miniature of Annette which is among his possessions;
to her cousin, M. de la Flotte, for the same autho-
risation as regards Paul Vallon's portrait, and also
for having been allowed to read the memoirs of his
grandfather Amédée Vallon, Paul's second son.

I am deeply grateful to Mr. Gordon Wordsworth,
the lineal descendant of the poet, for his courteous
communications and especially for his positive assurance that no traces of Annette and Caroline subsist
in the family papers that have been preserved, for
it would have been unjustifiable to give to the world
a fragmentary and often conjectural story of the
episode so long as there remained a possibility of
having a more thorough account of the poet's doings
and feelings.

It is a pleasant duty to express my thanks to
M. Guy Trouillard, already mentioned, and M.
Jacques Soyer, the Archivist of Loiret; to M. Pinault,

chef de l'État civil de Blois, whose inexhaustible kindness has allowed me to ascertain many facts and dates in the lives of the Vallons before 1815; and to Mademoiselle Cécile Ducaffy of the " Archives Départementales et Communales, Préfecture de la Seine," to whose untiring and intelligent exertions I owe the discovery of the living descendants of Wordsworth and Annette.

Yet, in spite of so much benevolent aid and of my personal efforts, I am conscious that much still remains obscure in the story. The course of the love story of Annette and William in France can be better imagined than historically related. It is therefore pleasant to hear that it will soon be told with the enviable freedom of the novelist by Mrs. Margaret Woods. The biographer is often at a loss: it is impossible for him to say exactly what took place at Orleans and what at Blois. Neither is it known with certainty whether Wordsworth took the bold step of revisiting France and Annette in the midst of the Terror. The feelings and conversations of the two former lovers at Calais in 1802 can only be guessed at; so can the help given by the poet to the mother either to educate or marry their daughter.

Those questions would, of course, be clearly answered, had not the poet's nephew and first biographer done away with all the papers and letters relating to the adventure. It was surely his right, and he considered it his duty, to do so. But it happens that by so doing he perhaps suppressed what might be to-day Wordsworth's best justification, or at any rate what might account for some things which we can either not explain or not approve.

It is to be hoped that the too meagre lineaments of the story as told in this book will be little by little filled up by new documents, the existence or whereabouts of which the writer had not the means of imagining.

The substance of the following pages is nearly identical with the articles in the *Revue des Deux Mondes*. But the limited space allowed him in the Review having obliged the author to compress or suppress several details, he now takes the opportunity of publishing his text at full length. All the references lacking in the Review will be found here. Several documents of various interest have also been given in full in the Appendices, instead of the short extracts or mere analyses as hitherto. Moreover, some illustrations are now added: besides Wordsworth's well-known portrait by Hancock about 1796, they consist of the reproduction of a miniature which is presumed by the Vallon family to represent Annette under the Directory; the portrait of Wordsworth's daughter Caroline in her old age, and for comparison that of Wordsworth by Haydon about 1830; the likeness of Paul Vallon, who plays an important part in the story of his sister's life; and finally the facsimile of a page of the letter written by Annette to Wordsworth in 1793, and confiscated by the French police.

It is perhaps superfluous to vindicate the present book against the charge of being one of those unpleasant disclosures which the public would be better without, for the subject it deals with is no longer secret. Wordsworth's youthful irregularity is now well known, and it is my sincere belief that his reputation will suffer less damage if the tale is

told at full length. What he might now most suffer
from, would be timid reticence and whispered hints.
Many a reader will even admit that the man's
honest nature is made more manifest by the long
fight of his loyalty against untoward circumstances.
More humanised and truer to life, he may become
more sympathetic in the end. It is good to know
that he did not find sanctity ready-made in his cradle,
and that no privilege of nature made easier for him
than for others the unfailing practice of the domestic
virtues which he was to celebrate in some of his
best verse. The character shown by the beginning
of this story was a real young man, not a premature
sage. He was altogether like the lover of Ruth:

> . . . A Youth to whom was given
> So much of earth—so much of Heaven,
> And such impetuous blood.

But the following pages are not only intended to
complete the likeness of a great poet on whom so
many books have already been written. It has also
appeared to me that the French family he chanced
to be connected with had a striking story well
deserving notice; that their adventures were much
the same in outline as many of those novels of Balzac
whose characters follow the fluctuations of the most
dramatic, most intense and unstable period of French
annals; that, in fact, it was upon the destinies of
such families that more than one volume of the
" Comédie Humaine " was built up. The mysterious
conspiracies, wild intrigues and police inquiries so
dear to Balzac are not wanting in the lives of the
Vallons. But in this instance, the singularity of such
eventful lives is made more striking by the propin-
quity of a great foreign poet, of the solitary dreamer

of the Lakes and august priest of Nature, who was at one time almost sucked in by their vortex. One wonders at the convergence of his hermit life with their tumultuous careers. The mere contrast is enough to make one admire the variety and picturesqueness of this world.

WILLIAM WORDSWORTH

AND

ANNETTE VALLON

I

WHEN William Wordsworth arrived at Orleans at the beginning of December 1791, he was twenty-one and a half years old. Though he had taken his degree in January, he still postponed, in spite of the entreaties of his uncles and guardians, the choice of his career. Yet his means were limited. At that time, his sister Dorothy estimated that she and her brothers possessed £470 each, but that the cost of William's education had to be deducted from his share.[1] He then possessed only the bare means of staying some months in France in very modest circumstances. It is true that all the orphans had one hope: that of the recovery of a considerable sum of money owed to their father by the Earl of Lonsdale whose steward he had been: a dangerous hope which induced in the young poet a tendency to idle away his time in waiting, to shirk definite tasks, and follow his wandering instincts. At the moment of his arrival in France he had found a pretext for procrastination: he was aiming, so he said, at a thorough knowledge of French so as to fit himself to be tutor

[1] Harper's *William Wordsworth, His Life, Works and Influence*, London, 1916, Vol. I. p. 87.

to some rich young fellow-countryman, and to
accompany him in his continental travels. At the
back of his mind was a desire to gain time, to escape
from drudgery and to write poetry. Who was to say,
after all, whether the poems he was even then com-
posing, were not to make him famous at once, sparing
him the slavery of a profession? He was revising
a description of his birthplace, the beautiful Lake
Country,[1] and meditating another [2] of the splendid
Alpine tramp he had made the year before with a
Cambridge friend, on foot, his knapsack on his back.

In all these verses Nature is his theme. His
dominant passion had already revealed itself, but it
was still far from engrossing all his thoughts. He
was curious of everything; he felt a keen appetite for
life. His mood was not yet attuned to the seclusion
of a country hermitage. Hardly out of college, he had
settled in London where he had just spent several
months, idling about, drawn thither by the varied
pleasures of the crowded metropolis, and if he now
turned to France, the principal attraction was the Revolution. He remembered his arrival at Calais on 13th
July, 1790, the eve of the Federation, and the ecstasy
of joy and hope that then possessed the whole country:
a thrilling memory which long made his heart beat
faster, and the traces of which he sought during
his new stay. His mind still bore the imprint of
those ineffable hours during which the rapture of a
whole nation had accompanied with its mighty music
his own mirth of a student on holiday. His mind
was then stirred by no political faith, unless it were
by the word Liberty in its fresh gloss, its vague-
ness full of infinite promise; he had, above all, been

[1] *An Evening Walk.*   [2] *Descriptive Sketches.*

moved by the overflowing spirit of brotherhood that showed itself in a thousand acts of courtesy towards the young Englishman, the son of a free country. Decidedly the glimpse he had had of France and of the French had enchanted him.

He now returned eager to enjoy that same hearty greeting, and with his expectations of social intercourse he could not but mingle some dream of love, the scenes and circumstances of which he could not yet determine. Everything predisposed him to it. No existing attachment was there to prevent a new passion; no strict rule of conduct yet guided his steps. Austerity had been foreign to his education; for this he was grateful all his life, rejoicing to have been

> Unchecked by innocence too delicate,
> And moral notions too intolerant,
> Sympathies too contracted.[1]

He had known no rigid discipline in his native Westmorland, still less at Cambridge, loose as its morals were. He does not conceal from us that at the university he consorted with *bons vivants* rather than with earnest students. It is saying a good deal, and will suggest much to those who have read to some extent the descriptions of college life in those days.

It may not be superfluous to remind the reader that Wordsworth was born in 1770, so that he was an old man of 67 when Queen Victoria ascended the throne. He might have died before her accession without any loss to his poetry and to his glory. It is only through his latest, and weakest, effusions and

---

[1] *Prelude*, XIV. 339–41.

B

chiefly owing to the tendency of his first biographers that he has assumed that Victorian air which is decidedly anachronistic. No greater mistake can be made in literary history than the confusion of the two epochs, the one in which he lived and the one in which he outlived himself and died. Wordsworth was, to all intents and purposes, a Georgian throughout his best years, and his youthful conduct should be judged according to the standard of times very widely separated from those of Victoria.

Great looseness of manners prevailed in the last decades of the eighteenth century—much corruption in the higher and much roughness in the lower ranks of society. There certainly existed even then in England, chiefly among the Evangelicals, classes of men remarkable for their entire purity—even austerity—of morals, but the general tone of the country was neither refined, nor even what would afterwards have been called simply decent.

Of the difference between those and later times, a single instance will suffice here. It puts, I think, the whole contrast in a nutshell. Dorothy Wordsworth, the poet's exquisite sister, writing to a friend in 1795—she was then twenty-three—expressed herself in this way:

A natural daughter of Mr. Tom Myers (a cousin of mine whom I dare say you have heard me mention) is coming over to England . . . to be educated . . . and T. Myers' brother . . . has requested that I should take her under my care.[1]

Who could imagine a young lady of the Victorian era speaking with this simplicity and ingenuousness

---

[1] Harper's *William Wordsworth*, I. p. 275.

of her cousin's natural daughter? This is only a trifling example of the unconventionality of those days, but it tends to show to what an extent natural children were a normal occurrence under the Georges. The case was so usual that it scarcely provoked any comment.

There was no strain of asceticism in the young poet's nature, to make him an exception to his age. However reticent his poetry may be, we can feel in it the ardour of his blood in those years. It partly reveals what De Quincey bluntly describes as Words-worth's " preternatural animal sensibility, diffused through *all* the animal passions (or appetites) " and considers as the basis of his " intellectual passions." [1] It would be quite idle to give proofs, had not the fact been ignored by most critics and biographers. Setting aside the mysterious Lucy whom he was to sing in his finest verse and for whom he felt among the English hills " the joy of his desire," there were daughters of Westmorland farmers whom he visited during his Cambridge vacations. With them the whole night sometimes passed in dances from which he came home with fevered brain, having felt in their company

> Slight shocks of young love-liking interspersed,
> Whose transient pleasure mounted to the head
> And tingled through the veins.[2]

And it was that very " tingling " that had favoured the birth of his poetic vocation. It was in the morning following one of those nights of rustic

[1] *De Quincey's Collected Writings*, Edited by David Masson, II. p. 246.
[2] *Prelude*, IV. 317–19.

revelry that coming home on foot and seeing the
rise of a glorious dawn, he had had the first con-
sciousness of his genius and dedicated himself to
the worship of Nature.[1] The tumult of his senses
had been the means of rousing his imaginative fire.
For the first time he had felt the truth of the profound maxim he uttered later on: " Feeling comes
in aid of feeling." [2]

One year later, when he journeyed across the Alps,
the sublimity of the mountains had not engrossed his
enthusiasm to the point of blinding him to the beauty
of the girls he met on his way. The dark Italian
maids he passed by on the shore of Lake Como had
stirred in him voluptuous desires, and he was to
remember them in that very year 1792, in lines full
of a sensuous exaltation which makes itself felt in
spite of the awkward and old-fashioned form of
the verse :

> Farewell! those forms that, in thy noon-tide shade,
> Rest, near their little plots of wheaten glade;
> Those steadfast eyes, that beating breasts inspire
> To throw the " sultry ray " of young Desire;
> Those lips, whose tides of fragrance come, and go,
> Accordant to the cheek's unquiet glow;
> Those shadowy breasts in love's soft light arrayed,
> And rising, by the moon of passion swayed.[3]

Surely the young man who wrote these lines
was neither ignorant of, nor deaf to the call of
the senses. He revelled in beautiful scenery but
desired love;—love in its integrity, not merely the
immediate satisfaction of a passing fancy, for his
heart was as impetuous as his senses. He carried

---

[1] *Prelude*, IV. 319–38.   [2] *Prelude*, XII. 269–70.
[3] *Descriptive Sketches*, 148–56.

into his attachments the " violence of affection " [1]
that endeared him to his sister Dorothy. There were
in his disposition all the elements which make for
a great passion.

II

THIS, then, was the young man who on his arrival
at Orleans alighted at " The Three Emperors " and
without delay went in quest of lodgings. He finally
decided on the rooms offered him by Monsieur
Gellet-Duvivier, a hosier, Rue Royale, at the corner
of the Rue du Tabour which is called the Coin-
Maugas. There, for the moderate sum of eighty
francs a month, he had both board and lodging.[2]
His host was a man of 37 whose mind had been
deranged by his wife's recent death, and who showed
imprudent exaltation in the expression of his hatred
of the Revolution,—an unfortunate whose tragic end
we shall soon hear of. In his house the poet found
as fellow-boarders two or three cavalry officers, and
a young gentleman from Paris, who all no doubt
shared the political opinions of their host. When
he wrote on the 19th December to his elder brother
he knew as yet no one else in the town.

Yet there was one exception : " one family which
I find very agreeable, and with which I became
acquainted by the circumstance of going to look at
their lodgings, which I should have liked extremely

[1] Letter of Dorothy of 16th Feb., 1793.
[2] Letter to Richard Wordsworth, 19th Dec., 1791. Harper,
I. p. 145.

to have taken, but I found them too dear for me."
Here the paper is torn and we can only make out the
words: "I have . . . of my evenings there." Does
he mean that being unable to lodge with them he
was spending his evenings at their house? And was
that house the house in which Annette was living?
And if such is the case, is it the house in the Rue
du Poirier where lived M. André Augustin Dufour,
greffier du tribunal of the Orleans district, who with
his wife was to assist Annette in her ordeal?

Mere conjectures these, to which we are driven
by the lack of authentic details. The letter to his
brother Richard, in which Wordsworth gives us
these few details, is cheerful. We feel that he is
enjoying the novelty of the place. Everything pleases
him; even the surrounding country, which no doubt
seems very flat to the hill-born youth, but abounds
"in agreeable walks, especially by the side of the
Loire, which is a very magnificent river."

He realises that his French is not at all up to the
mark, yet he does not intend to engage a teacher of
the language. He has no intention of going to that
expense. Had he, so soon, found Annette willing to
give him free conversation lessons?

The young lady whose life was to be linked with
his own, Marie Anne (or Annette) Vallon, was born
at Blois on 22nd June, 1766. She was the sixth and
last child of Jean Léonard, surnamed Vallon, a
surgeon, and of Françoise Yvon, his wife. The
father belonged to a family which, by its own tradition, traced itself back to Scotland, and in which the
surgical profession was hereditary. One of Annette's
brothers, writing to the Board of the Hôtel-Dieu of
Blois, stated that his great-grandfather, grandfather

and father had been surgeons of the same hospital in succession. In 1755, at the funeral of Joseph Léonard Vallon, formerly surgeon, aged 95, the chief mourner was the " Sieur Vallon," his son, himself *maître chirurgien*. It appears that Jean, Annette's father, was a grandson of the aged Joseph Léonard. Her two eldest brothers, Jean Jacques, born in 1758, and Charles Henry, born the following year, adopted the paternal profession. They were both attached as surgeons to the Hôtel-Dieu before 1792.

When Wordsworth made Annette's acquaintance, the girl's father had been dead for several years and her mother had married again, her second husband being a " Sieur Vergez," himself a surgeon. Father-less, somehow morally estranged from her mother by the latter's re-marriage, Annette was hardly less left to herself than William.

In addition to the two surgeons who were the eldest sons of the family, there was yet a third— Paul, born in 1763, who had turned his thoughts to law. Also three daughters: Françoise Anne, born in 1762; Angélique Adélaïde, born in 1765; and Marie Anne, one year younger, the latest born.

Two second cousins of the children are also known to us: Charles Olivier and Claude Léonnar (*sic*) Vallon, born the first in 1728 and the other in 1729, both *curés* of the diocese of Blois, both reconciled with the Revolution and patronised by the constitutional Bishop Grégoire, who made Claude one of his *vicaires épiscopaux* in the department of Loir-et-Cher. They had taken the constitutional oath in 1791; they were in the autumn of 1792 to take the oath of *liberté-égalité*; and five years later, on 30th Fructidor of the fifth Republican year, that

of hatred to monarchy. For these reasons a pre-
fectorial report of 9th Thermidor of the ninth
year of the Republic speaks highly of them.   It
commends Claude's " great theological science " and
declares Charles to be " of perfect morals, learned
and tolerant." [1]

There does not seem, then, to have prevailed from
the first in the Vallon family the hostility towards
the Revolution which manifested itself later on so
violently in some of their members. The name of
Jean Jacques, given in 1758 to the eldest of Annette's
brothers, strengthens this impression. The father
must have become an adept of the new creed spread
by Jean Jacques Rousseau; of his worship of nature
and sensibility.   Yet there was a sturdy sense of
tradition in that well-established family whose head
had for generation after generation confined himself
within his corporation as within a caste. If the two
priests themselves became " constitutional," they
none the less retained their loyalty to religion.
Charles Olivier uttered an indignant protest when
the Convention, in order to sever priests from Chris-
tianity, pledged itself to give pecuniary assistance to
those who would be willing to give up the ministry.
He wrote to the *Citoyen Administrateur* on 30th
March, 1794, the very day on which Robespierre
ordered the arrest of the *Indulgents*: " I beg you
will not depend on me for help, and not take it ill
if I tell you truthfully that religion, conscience and
honour forbid me to take any step towards resigning
my ministry, which I hold from God alone." [2]   He

[1] I owe my information on the two priests to Abbé J.
Gallerand, professor at the Seminary of Blois.

[2] Letter communicated to me by Madame Lecoq-Vallon.

was in the end, after the Concordat, to recant his oaths of the revolutionary period.

Finally Wordsworth's evidence, his repeated affirmation in *The Prelude* that, before knowing Captain Michel Beaupuy, he had lived among the opponents of the Revolution, induces us to think that as early as 1792 those of the Vallon family whose acquaintance he could have made, saw rather with sorrow than with satisfaction the advance of the nation towards a republic. As to Annette herself, it is probable that she remained rather indifferent to politics until the day when a tragedy that struck her home threw her into the most active opposition. If she felt the slightest disagreement with Wordsworth's opinions on monarchy and republic, it did not trouble her much, engrossed as she was by her love for him.

III

UNLESS we are to accept the idea that Annette became Wordsworth's mistress on their very first meeting, the birth of their child as early as 15th December, 1792, obliges us to think they made each other's acquaintance soon after the poet's arrival at Orleans where he spent the winter.[1] There is nothing

---

[1] It is impossible to know the exact date of Wordsworth's change of residence from Orleans to Blois, but we know that he meant to spend the winter in the former town (Letter to Mathews of 23rd Nov., 1791, Harper, I. p. 122, and Dorothy's of 7th Dec., 1791, *ibid.* p. 124). On the other hand, if we admit that there is a parallelism between his own story and that of *Vaudracour and Julia,* we are led to infer that Wordsworth's love had two successive towns for its scene of action.

astonishing in Annette having made a stay—even a prolonged stay—in that town. In Orleans lived her brother Paul, with whom she seems to have been particularly intimate, partly, perhaps, on account of their nearness in age, partly on account of a certain similarity of temperament. Paul had for some years been notary's clerk in Orleans under a Maître Courtois, whose office was in the Rue de Bourgogne, close to the Rue du Poirier where the Dufours were living. In winter Orleans offered more attractions, being a larger and busier town. Paul had made friends there, and his worldly tastes, his sociable temper, found an echo in Annette.

We know what Paul's physical appearance was: he was a small dark man, with a thick-set neck, and large bold eyes under heavy black brows. We have a glimpse of his character in the memoirs of his grandson Amédée, a magistrate, who declares him to have been " one of the wittiest men he had the privilege of knowing," with an excellent heart. His chivalry and generosity tended to excess, and his carelessness of money was so great that his financial position suffered by it. The appearance of Annette's daughter is also known to us. It is a face which, according to its age, wears a look of frank gaiety, or a gently mischievous smile. But Annette dwells so much on her daughter's likeness to her father that it would be illusory to expect to find the expression of the mother in the face of the child. The portrait of Annette published in this volume is not well enough authenticated for us to place much reliance on it. It does not seem as if liveliness had been outstandingly characteristic of her, though kindness and generosity certainly were. In the letters of

Annette that have recently been discovered the dominant note is that of an irrepressible, exuberant sensibility which is a trait of her nature and is not exclusively due to the harassing circumstances in which the letters were written. She abounded in words, was prone to effusions and tears. These emotions of a " sensitive soul " were, moreover, quite of a nature to win her the young Englishman's heart. He himself was in those years inclined to melancholy and the elegiac mood. His very first sonnet [1] had been inspired by the sight of a girl weeping at the hearing of a woeful story. At that sight, he said, his blood had stopped running in his veins:

> Dim were my swimming eyes—my pulse beat slow,
> And my full heart was swell'd to dear delicious pain.

The maiden's tears had made manifest her virtue. The poet's turn for sentimentality found in Annette many an opportunity of satisfying itself, while the garrulity of the young Frenchwoman fell in splendidly with his intention of learning the language.

All subsequent evidence agrees in representing Annette as obliging and generous. For economy's sake, Wordsworth had decided on not incurring the expense of a teacher. Annette, then, was his tutor. She listened kindly to the stammered sentences of the foreigner. She set him at ease by laughing good-humouredly over his unpronounceable name. Her tender heart was filled with affection for the youth,

[1] Sonnet signed *Axiologus*, printed in *European Magazine* (March 1787) and ascribed to Wordsworth by Knight and Hutchinson. Professor Harper expresses some doubt as to the authorship.

younger than she by four and a half years, who was separated from all his friends and was living among men whose language he knew but ill. And when William allowed his budding passion to burst forth, her too charitable soul was powerless against his ardour.

His love for her was an exalted, blinding passion, in the presence of which all else vanished. The sight of Annette at her window, or even of Annette's window alone, was each day's supreme instant. He himself tells us so, though under a disguise, in the story of *Vaudracour and Julia*.

A wretched poem, said Matthew Arnold, the only one of Wordsworth's which it was impossible for him to read. The verdict is not altogether unde-served. But Arnold errs in not excepting a few very fine lines, and, on the other hand, does not take into account what we now know, that is to say the keen biographical interest of this awkward and confused poem, to which the author seems to have found some difficulty in assigning a place amongst his works, and of which he is at a loss to explain the origin.

He began by inserting it at the end of the very book of *The Prelude* in which his memories of France are related. The poem strikes the love note which is lacking elsewhere. It was at first, according to Wordsworth, a story told by his friend Captain Beaupuy, the devoted Republican, who was trying to make the young Englishman realise the evils of the old regime, and particularly the horrors of the *lettres de cachet*.

Young Vaudracour, a nobleman from Auvergne, loved a daughter of the people whom he wanted to marry. A *lettre de cachet* obtained by his father came as a barrier between him and his purpose. Imprisoned for having killed one of the men sent out to arrest him, he only recovered his freedom by pledging himself to give up his mistress. Could he be true to such an oath? The lovers met again, but were again violently separated. Julia, now a mother, was shut up in a convent. The child was left with Vaudracour, who withdrew with it to a hermitage in the woods. 1789 sounded the call of freedom; it could not rouse him from his lethargy: he had become insane.

It is easy to see that Vaudracour is not Wordsworth, nor his story that of the poet. There existed between Wordsworth and Annette no difference of caste. The surgeon's daughter was as good as the son of the Earl of Lonsdale's steward. There was no violence used in their case; no *lettre de cachet*, murder, prison, convent, nor tragic ending. But before coming to the lovers' woes, the poet described *con amore*—and it is the only place in his works where he has done so—the intoxication of passion. As invention never was his *forte*, he turned for help to the memories and exact circumstances of his own love-story in order to give some reality to the first hours of rapture broken by sudden partings. He may have been afraid lest marks of his personality should be discovered in the poem if it found a place so near his own adventures, and it is this, rather than the over-burdening of the Ninth Book of *The Prelude*, and the awkwardness of its composition—he never was very sensitive to defects of this kind—which induced him to publish *Vaudracour and Julia* separately in 1804. Later on, when in his old age he started commenting upon his poems, he wrote at the head of this one a note, the object of which was to avert suspicion, rather than to give information to the public. The story, he says this time, was told him not by Beaupuy but " from the mouth of a French lady who had been an eye-and-ear-witness of all that was done and said." And he adds: " The facts are true; no invention as to these has been exercised, as none was needed."

A most astonishing French lady surely, with the eyes of a lynx, the ears of a mole, to have overheard, even to their minutest details, all the lovers' effusions, and to have been both present and invisible at their most secret meetings! One can hardly refrain from smiling, in reading the beginning of the poem, at the thought of the story-teller endowed with senses so acute behind whom the poet hides his identity.

However, no careful reader will be led astray. Professor Harper, the most thorough and best informed of his biographers, straightway proclaimed the connection between *Vaudracour and Julia*, and Wordsworth's youthful love adventure. The real difficulty is to draw the line between reality and fiction, between Wordsworth's story and Vaudracour's.

To Wordsworth, the lover of Annette, no doubt belong the ecstasies of the very young man who sees, not a mere woman of flesh and blood, but rather he knows not what blinding splendour: " . . . He beheld a vision and adored the thing he saw," a vision so dazzling that its very radiance renders it indistinct. It will be observed that his attitude of wonder is more in keeping with the youth's sudden passion for the foreigner, than with Vaudracour's long and tender love for his Julia, known from the cradle, beloved since she was a child, the constant companion of his games throughout his childhood.

Let us listen to the poet:

> Arabian fiction never filled the world
> With half the wonders that were wrought for him.
> Earth breathed in one great presence of the spring;
> Life turned the meanest of her implements,
> Before his eyes, to price above all gold;
> The house she dwelt in was a sainted shrine;
> Her chamber-window did surpass in glory
> The portals of the dawn; all Paradise
> Could, by the simple opening of a door,
> Let itself in upon him:—pathways, walks,
> Swarmed with enchantment, till his spirit sank,
> Surcharged, within him, overblest to move
> Beneath a sun that wakes a weary world
> To its dull round of ordinary cares;
> A man too happy for Mortality!

These were the first days of fascination, when the lovers were still innocent.

In comparison with that—for him exceptional—outburst, the story of the consummation of their love is cold and stilted, and full of awkward explanations that seem to chill the lover's ardour:

> So passed the time, till, whether through effect
> Of some unguarded moment that dissolved
> Virtuous restraint—oh, speak it, think it, not!
> Deem rather that the fervent Youth, who saw
> So many bars between his present state
> And the dear haven where he wished to be
> In honourable wedlock with his Love,
> Was in his judgment tempted to decline
> To perilous weakness, and entrust his cause
> To nature for a happy end of all;
> Deem that by such fond hope the Youth was swayed
> And bear with their transgression, when I add
> That Julia, wanting yet the name of wife,
> Carried about her for a secret grief
> The promise of a mother. . . .

Poor verse and wretched moral! Rather than confess to the rash thoughtlessness of an instant of passion, to the sudden exaltation of heart and senses, the poet chooses to ascribe to Vaudracour a calculated act, in the very depth of his transports. In spite of that constrained explanation, suggested with but little conviction by the author himself, we are tempted to believe that Wordsworth and Annette merely succumbed, with no preconceived design, like thousands of others, because nature prevailed over prudence, and passion over wisdom. They loved each other unreservedly from the time of their stay at Orleans; and when Annette left the town to go back to Blois, at the beginning of the spring of 1792, she already carried about her, like Julia, perhaps not knowing it, perhaps not yet being sure of it, " the promise of a mother."

IV

SHALL we look in *Vaudracour and Julia* for the reason of that change of residence? Vaudracour is opposed not only by his father but also by Julia's humble parents, who are in fear of the nobleman's anger. Julia, as soon as her shame is known to them, is hurried away by them one night, in spite of her protests. When in the morning her lover realises what has happened, he does not know whither to turn for her. He

. . . Chafed like a wild beast in the toils.

But he is soon able to find her track, follows her to the distant town where they carried and confined her :

Easily may the sequel be divined—
Walks to and fro—watchings at every hour;
And the fair Captive, who, whene'er she may,
Is busy at her casement as the swallow
Fluttering its pinions, almost within reach,
About the pendent nest, did thus espy
Her Lover!—thence a stolen interview,
Accomplished under friendly shade of night.

Was Annette in the same way taken back to Blois in spite of herself and torn from her lover by her alarmed friends? We have no reason for assuming this. Her father was dead. Her mother, who had married again, was without much power over her. Yet Blois was her native town; there stood the family house. She had no private means and had probably visited Orleans on the invitation of friends or her brother Paul, for a limited space of time. Despite her twenty-five years, she was therefore still partly dependent on her people, and it is likely that at Blois the couple's intimacy was held in greater check than at Orleans. The town was smaller and Annette better looked after.

Indeed the two lovers *did* wander about Blois and its surroundings. We even know that their walks often took them to the neighbourhood of the convent in which Annette had been brought up—an opportunity for them to grow sentimental over " their happy innocent years." [1]   For aught we know, Wordsworth may have had some access to the Vallon family. He may have been acquainted with the two priests, the uncles of Annette, who were perhaps in his mind when he said to Ellis Yarnall in 1849, that during the Revolution " he had

[1] We gather this from Annette's letter printed in Appendix II.

C

known many of the *abbés* and other ecclesiastics, and
thought highly of them as a class; they were earnest,
faithful men; being unmarried, he must say, they
were the better able to fulfil their sacred duties;
they were married to their flocks." [1]

But it is not certain how far the house in which
Annette lived was open to the young man. We are
therefore inclined to believe that Wordsworth drew
from his own memories the lines—the last fine lines
of the poem—in which he describes a nocturnal
meeting of the lovers, invoking for the occasion the
memory of Romeo and Juliet, and of the lark which
gave the signal for the last embrace. This scene of
passion on a summer night, which the French lady
narrator could surely not have seen with her eyes
nor heard with her ears, probably commemorates
one of their secret meetings during the second part
of their loves:

> . . . Through all her courts
> The vacant city slept; the busy winds,
> That keep no certain intervals of rest,
> Moved not; meanwhile the galaxy displayed
> Her fires, that like mysterious pulses beat
> Aloft;—momentous but uneasy bliss!
> To their full hearts the universe seemed hung
> On that brief meeting's slender filament!

[1] Reminiscences of Mr. Ellis Yarnall of Philadelphia: W.
Knight's *Life of Wordsworth*, Vol. II. p. 334. The passage
immediately preceding is amusing, read in the light of what we
now know. "France," relates Yarnall, "was our next subject,
and one which seemed very near his heart. He had been
much in that country at the outbreak of the Revolution, and
afterwards during its wildest excesses. At the time of the
September massacres he was at Orleans. *Addressing Mrs.
Wordsworth, he said : ' I wonder I came to stay there so long,
and at a period so exciting.'* "

The other striking fact of Wordsworth's stay at Blois, the town of the Vallons, is his friendship with Captain Beaupuy. Of that attachment only, he spoke abundantly and beautifully in his *Prelude*. But in omitting Annette, he at the same time did away with all that made the pathetic complexity of those summer months.

Wordsworth, who could now see Annette only by stealth, found himself thrown back upon the society of other companions. It seems that at this time he was boarding with officers of the late Bassigny regiment, all of whom, with one exception, he introduces to us as exalted aristocrats whose minds were bent on emigrating. He now made friends with the only one who was in favour of the new ideas, Captain Michel Beaupuy. Very soon, their friendship became close, and the young foreigner deferentially listened to the officer of thirty-seven who—a nobleman by birth—had abandoned all the interests of his caste and even the esteem of his colleagues for the revolutionary cause. Beaupuy's eager proselytism converted the young Englishman into a true patriot,—a *Jacobin* in the sense the word had in 1792—prompted by a zeal equal to his own. They were frequently to be seen together at the patriotic club of Blois;[1] in the town and its surroundings, among neighbouring forests and even in places as distant as Chambord or Vendôme, they would take long walks during which Beaupuy preached his gospel. From each of these talks, Wordsworth returned increasingly exalted by his republican enthusiasm, for a Republic was in

[1] See Harper's *Life of William Wordsworth*, Vol. I. ch. viii., and especially his "Wordsworth at Blois" in *John Morley and other Essays*, 1920.

the air. His ardour was like a consuming fever. In that heart already heated by love, stirred by anxiety and remorse, it soon flamed into passion. Again "feeling comes in aid of feeling." Meanwhile Annette was beginning secretly to prepare the expected baby's linen, bidding William touch and kiss all the things that were to be used for the infant, particularly "a little pink cap" intended for it. They mourned together, between two kisses, their lost innocence. Dreading the impending and inevitable revelations, they discussed, perhaps, the possibility of a marriage that would patch up matters. In these impassioned emotions, weeks passed away and the much dreaded event drew nearer.

V

BEAUPUY had started for the Rhine on 27th July with his regiment, and Wordsworth still lingered at Blois. Beaupuy had not been the cause of his coming there, and he needed another departure, another invitation to go away in his turn. He stayed on till the beginning of September, and we may hazard two reasons for his new removal.

One of them may have been the sudden death of Annette's eldest brother. Jean Jacques the surgeon died at thirty-four, leaving a widow and two little daughters, one aged two years and the other a few months. According to a family tradition, he was killed one night in the forest of Blois on his way to bring urgent help to a wounded man. The precise date is missing, but would appear to be in the second

half of 1792. For the benefit of his widow, three
doctors from Blois offered to the town officials to
take over his post as surgeon to the Hôtel-Dieu and
to the hospitals of the parishes of St. Louis, St.
Nicolas and St. Saturnin. One of the three was his
own brother Charles Henry, who, at the widow's
request, was finally appointed on 13th November.[1]
Such a tragedy alone would have been sufficient to
upset the family and necessitate some changes. But
Annette's departure from Blois may easily be accounted for by direct motives. The state she was
in could no longer be concealed. It was impossible
for her to remain in her native town without her
trouble becoming public. She preferred to return
to Orleans where, in some quiet place near com-
passionate friends, she might give birth to her child.
And Wordsworth again followed her thither. On 3rd
September, he once more dated from Blois a letter
to his elder brother, asking him for an urgently
needed sum of money. The next day he was back
at Orleans, where he tells us he happened to be
during the September massacres.

It was indeed on the morning of 4th September
that Fournier, surnamed the American, despite the
orders issued by the Convention, started at the head
of his gang for Versailles with the prisoners who
were waiting in the prison of Orleans for the verdict
of the " High Court." At Versailles, *septembrisseurs*
(or assassins) from Paris were appointed to meet and
butcher them. This crime, conceived and perpe-
trated in cold blood, caused a shudder of horror
to run through the town which had witnessed the

[1] Archives of the Hôtel-Dieu of Blois, Registre E³, folios
57-8.

wretched creatures' departure. It left behind an inextinguishable hatred in the hearts of all those who were not among the fanatics of the Republic. It is astonishing that Wordsworth should make no allusion to this event; he speaks of the September massacres only as of a Parisian tragedy. The only event he commemorates, either in his *Descriptive Sketches* or in his *Prelude*, as having taken place during the period of his second stay at Orleans is the proclamation of the Republic. This is the occasion of a veritable pæan of joy. His *Sketches* show him wandering by the source of the Loiret and seeing the river, its banks and the whole earth transformed by the magic world. It is all over with the monarchy, with all monarchies. The reign of happiness and freedom has begun for all men.[1]

Strange alternations of enthusiasm and despondency when from those delightful visions he fell back to the thought of the young girl who was on the eve of becoming a mother. Was he allowed to see her at Orleans during the few weeks he spent

[1] On that same occasion, Wordsworth was probably present at the " Civic Feast " given at Orleans on 21st September to celebrate the suppression of monarchy, during which deputy Manuel made a speech before the Assembly. As a symbol of the fall of royalty, fire was set to a big wood-pile: " Le feu est solennellement mis à l'énorme bûcher, composé de fagots élevés en une haute pyramide couronnée d'un bouquet d'artifice qui bientôt tombe en mille flammèches étincelantes, et les citoyens se livrent à la joie qu'ils ressentent de l'établissement de la République française; dans leur enthousiasme, avec ces élans qui n'appartiennent qu'à des hommes vraiment dignes de la liberté, les cris de ' Vive la République! Vive la nation française! ' éclatent de toutes parts."—Quoted in *Histoire de la ville d'Orléans*, by Bimbenet, Vol. II. p. 1225.

there? He was to leave Orleans at the end of October for Paris and stay there for about two months. We know nothing of the reasons of these comings and goings. It is certain, however, that he lingered in France beyond the appointed date. On 3rd October he again informed his elder brother of his proposed return to London in the course of the month. But what motive prompted him to leave Orleans before Annette's deliverance? Was his presence considered inadvisable in view of the secrecy that was desired? On the other hand, he could not bring himself to put the sea between himself and Annette so long as he did not know the now imminent issue.

It was in Paris that he learned the birth of his daughter. On 15th December, 1792, in the cathedral church of Sainte Croix, was baptised " Anne Caroline Wordswodsth (sic), daughter of Williams Wordswodsth, Anglois, and of Marie Anne Vallon." Paul Vallon stood godfather to the child and Madame Augustin Dufour stood godmother. The absent father was represented by André Augustin Dufour, with a legal power from the poet. The father owned the child as his and gave it his name, in so far at least as the episcopal *vicaire* Perrin could spell it.[1]

Some little time after, at the end of December, Wordsworth came back to England. It seems that he stayed in France to the utmost limit of his resources, and it was against his will that he went back to his country, " dragged " as he says " by a chain of harsh necessity." [2] But he suffers us to think

[1] The full certificate of Caroline's birth has been printed by Professor Harper in *Wordsworth's French Daughter*, Princeton University Press, 1921.

[2] *Prelude*, X. 222.

that his revolutionary zeal alone made him wish to stay on in France. Had it been possible for him, he tells us, he would have shared the Girondins' fortune: " made common cause with some who perished." [1] He hides from us the chief reason of his unwillingness to leave the country in which his child had just been born.

VI

WHY did Wordsworth leave France without marrying Annette? He had owned his daughter, why did he not legitimise her by making the mother his wife? Considering the passion which inflamed him in 1792, it seems he would have done so there and then, had it been in his power. And yet there was no marriage. There was none before Caroline's birth, as her christening certificate testifies; there was none later on, as is attested by the death certificate of Annette, who died a " spinster."

The likeliest explanation is his poverty, which was only too real. To support wife and child he needed help from his guardians, an instalment of the money that was to be his one day. Therefore it was indispensable to obtain their consent. He might perhaps disarm their opposition by showing his readiness to enter some one of the careers they pointed out to him—even the church, which, at that time, did not exact too strict a faith. He decided, therefore, to go to England, with the intention of returning shortly to bring help to the dear ones he had left in France,

[1] *Prelude*, X. 229–30.

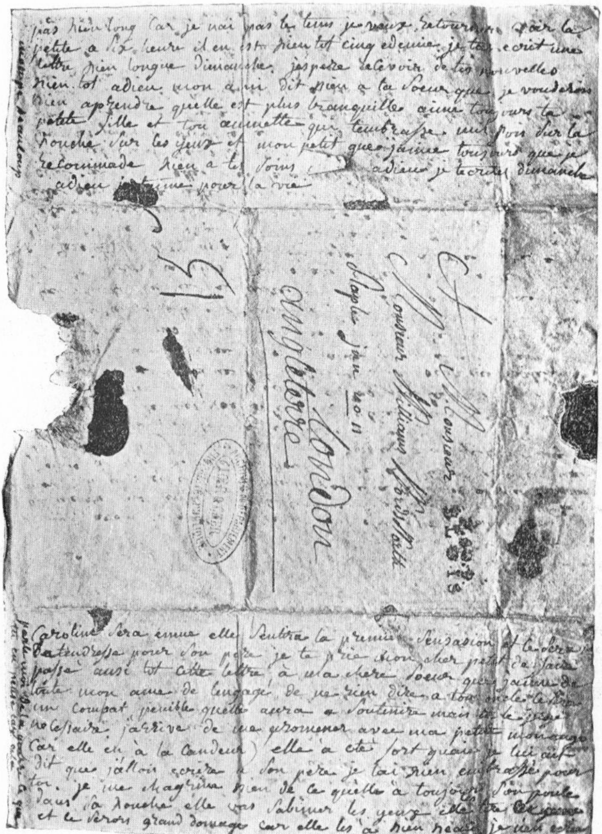
pas bien long car je n'ai pas le tems je veux retourner voir la
petite a six heure il en est bien tot cinq edemie je te ecrit une
lettre bien longue dimanche jespere recevoir de tes nouvelles
bien tot adieu mon ami dit bien a ta soeur que je voudrois
bien apprendre quelle est plus tranquille aime toujours ta
petite fille et ton annette qui tembrasse mil fois sur la
bouche sur les yeux et mon petit que jaime toujours que je
retournerai bien a tes soins [illegible] adieu je tecrirai dimanche
adieu je taime pour la vie

Monsieur
Monsieur Williams Wordsworth
Staple inn [illegible]
London
angleterre

Caroline sera emue elle sentira la premiere sensation de tendresse
de tendresse pour son pere je te prie mon cher petit de faire
passer aussi tot cette lettre a ma chere soeur que jaime de
toute mon ame de l'engager de ne rien dire a ton oncle [illegible]
un combat penible quelle aura a soutenir mais [illegible]
necessaire. jarrive de me promener avec ma petite mignonne
car elle en a la candeur) elle a été fort gaie je lui ai
dit que jallois ecrire a son pere je lai bien embrassé pour
toi. je me chagrine bien de ce quelle a toujours son pouce
dans sa bouche elle vas sabimer les yeux [illegible]
et ce seroit grand domage car elle les a bien beaux [illegible]

FACSIMILE OF A LETTER FROM ANNETTE VALLON

TO WILLIAM WORDSWORTH, 20TH MARCH, 1792

or to take them away with him to his own country. This plan was submitted to Annette, who accepted it resignedly. Wordsworth was to come back and marry her as soon as he had his guardians' consent and the necessary help.

Another man might have reversed the decision; married Annette straightway, then placed before his guardians the accomplished fact. Marriage first; money would come afterwards when fate should think fit. This would have been splendid imprudence, but it was made impossible by the inborn cautiousness of the young poet. His native wariness inclined to procrastination. Besides, he may have been somewhat alarmed by the force of the fascination which enchained him. To speak plainly, he had lived in France for months in an unknown, strange and feverish atmosphere in which he felt at times as though he were dreaming. Annette was fascinating, but she remained in part a mystery to him. He felt anxious at having so far resigned his will-power, and lost the control of his actions. She gave the impulse and swept him on in her wake, not merely because she was four years older than he, but because she was gifted with that natural intrepidity which was to make her a model conspirator, an "intriguer" as her political adversaries called her. Who can assert that she did not find pleasure in concealment, and in her very sorrows an exciting sensation not devoid of charm? Did Wordsworth in the depth of his heart feel a vague mistrust of the woman he loved?

VII

ON coming back to London, Wordsworth's time was occupied in two directions: the publication of his first two poems in the hope that they might bring him fortune as well as fame, and the consideration of the steps that must be taken to propitiate his uncles. He hesitated to face them, knowing them to be displeased and hostile. He begged his sister Dorothy, who lived with her uncle, Dr. Cookson, a clergyman, to speak for him. He confided everything to Dorothy, who immediately conceived a warm affection for the young French mother and her child. She imagined no other issue than marriage, and she already pictured the cottage in which the newly married couple would live, and in which she would have a place.[1] Of her own accord, she started

---

[1] We gather this from Annette's letters to William and Dorothy (Appendix II.). The dream of a retired life in a small cottage which is found both in Dorothy's letters and in Wordsworth's *Evening Walk* first makes its appearance at the beginning of 1793 when the letters were written and the poem published. It was first connected with William's determination to marry Annette. The cottage was to shelter both sister and wife. This is how we ought to read the following lines in *An Evening Walk*, addressed to Dorothy:

" Even now [Hope] decks for me a distant scene,
 (For dark and broad the gulf of time between)
 Gilding that cottage with her fondest ray,
 (Sole bourn, sole wish, sole object of my way;
 How fair its lawns and silvery woods appear!
 How sweet its streamlet murmurs in mine ear!)
 Where we, my Friend, to golden days shall rise,
 Till our small share of hardly-paining sighs
 (For sighs will ever trouble human breath)
 Creep hushed into the tranquil breast of death."

a correspondence with Annette, to whom she protested her sisterly affection. To carry on this letter-writing, she began "fagging at French again." But she trembled at the thought of telling the whole story to the Cooksons, whose anger she foresaw. She confessed her fear to Annette, who wrote to William: "I beg you to invite her not to say anything to your uncle. It will be a hard fight she will have to engage in. *But you deem it necessary*." And Annette forgot for a time her own grief in pitying Dorothy for the trouble she caused her. She was distressed at the thought of her being deprived of all sympathy:

> You have no one to whom you might freely confide the painful state of your soul, and you must check the tears which your tender feelings force from you. I advise you to hide as long as you possibly can from your uncle and aunt the reasons which make your tears flow.

Thus did Annette express herself in a double letter written on 20th March, 1793, to William and Dorothy, a letter seized by the French police on account of the war and recently discovered in the Blois Record Office.[1]

Annette returned to Blois with her child. She lived with her family, but for fear of scandal she had to part from Caroline, who was sent to a nurse some little way off in the suburbs, so that the poor mother might see her frequently. She carried on with Wordsworth a copious correspondence. If the letter to William dated 20th March is comparatively short, it is because she wrote "quite a long one" on the preceding Sunday, and because she is to write him another the Sunday following. It is also because

[1] See Appendix II.

she devotes hers this time chiefly to Dorothy, to whom she owes an answer and gives ample measure.

The two letters, read together, are a long and pathetic appeal to the distant friend. At every page is repeated the prayer: Come back and marry me. She suffers too much in his absence. She loves him so passionately! When she embraces her child, she thinks she holds William in her arms: "Her little heart often beats against mine; I think I am feeling her father's." She writes to Dorothy:

I wish I could give you some comfort, but alas! I cannot. I rather should look for it from you. It is in the certainty of your friendship that I find some comfort, and in the unalterable feelings of my dear Williams (*sic*). I cannot be happy without him, I long for him every day.

Indeed she sometimes tries to call reason to her help. She wishes for her lover's return, yet fears it, for war is threatening. She contradicts herself four times in the course of ten lines:

My distress would be lessened were we married, yet I regard it as almost impossible that you should risk yourself, if we should have war. You might be taken prisoner. But where do my wishes lead me? I speak as though the instant of my happiness were at hand. Write and tell me what you think, and do your very utmost to hasten your daughter's happiness and mine, but only if there is not the slightest risk to be run,—but I think the war will not last long. I should wish our two nations to be [reconciled]. That is one of my most earnest wishes. But above all, find out some way by which we can write to each other in case the correspondence between the two kingdoms were stopped.

Her strongest reason for insisting on marriage is her motherly love, rather than her wifely passion.

She is ready to accept that William should come only to go away again immediately afterwards, if he must. Although she needs him for her happiness she would make the sacrifice. But then her situation being regularised, her daughter could be given back to her. She writes to Dorothy:

I can assure you that were I happy enough to have my dear Williams journey back to France and give me the title of his wife, I should be comforted. First my daughter would have a father and her poor mother might enjoy the delight of always having her near. I should myself give her the care I am jealous to see her receive from other hands. I should no longer cause my family to blush by calling her my daughter, my Caroline; I should take her with me and go to the country. There is no solitude in which I should not find charm, being with her.

Her bitterest trial was on the day on which the child went out for the first time, for the woman who carried her passed before the mother's house without stopping: " That scene," she writes to Dorothy, " caused me a whole day of tears. They are flowing even now."

Indeed, Caroline is the theme of almost all her letters. She speaks endlessly about the wonderful progress achieved by the three-months-old babe. In her mother's eyes she is a beautiful picture of her father, though she is not fair-haired like him. Annette carries on with the child many a tender, childish dialogue. She smothers her with kisses and bathes her in tears. She speaks of her pride in dressing her, in putting on " that little pink cap which fits her so well," and which she had once bidden William kiss.

The first time she had it on, I put it on her head myself after kissing it a thousand times. I said to her,

" My Caroline, kiss this bonnet. Your father is less
happy than I; he cannot see it; but it should be dear
to you, for he put his lips to it."

The impression left on us by these letters is firstly,
that Annette is in every sense a kind and passionately
fond woman. No bitter word or recrimination is to be
found in all these pages. Nor is her disinterestedness
less manifest. She raises no cry of poverty, no call
for material help. She is all sensibility. Too much
so for our present taste, even if we take into account
the circumstances in which she writes. We feel that
her natural tenderness has been accentuated by the
reading of the novels of that time—novels in which
tears flowed abundantly, which teemed with moving
apostrophes. This is the more evident by reason of
the inferiority of her education. There is no punctuation in her letters and her spelling is eminently
fanciful. Here and there, one meets sentences with
a popular turn, like " le chagrin que vous avez *rap-
port à* moi "; then again we find whole paragraphs
overflowing with the facile sentimentality of the age.
She writes to Dorothy:

Often when I am alone in my room with his [William's]
letters, I dream he is going to walk in. I stand ready to
throw myself into his arms and say to him: " Come, my
love, come and dry these tears which have long been
flowing for you, let us fly and see Caroline, your child
and your likeness; behold your wife; sorrow has altered
her much; do you know her? Ay, by the emotion which
your heart must share with hers. If her features are altered,
if her pallor makes it impossible for you to know her, her
heart is unchanged. It is still yours. Know your Annette,
Caroline's tender mother. . . ." Ah! my dear sister,
such is my habitual state of mind. But waking from my

delusion as from a dream, I do not see him, my child's
father; he is very far from me. These transports occur
again and again, and throw me into a state of extreme
dejection.

Although inexhaustibly voluble when she pours
out her heart, she seems to be devoid of intellectual
curiosity. She is an afflicted lover, a doting mother.
But she seems to know nothing of that William whom
she longs to see again, nor yet to want to learn
anything. She does not inquire after his doings;
does she even realise that he is a poet? Of the war,
of politics, of the dawning Terror she has not a word
to say, except in so far as it concerns her lover's
journey. Her sentimental absorption is absolute.
The pathetic strain never relaxes.

One may imagine Wordsworth's perturbation as
he received these moving letters, which at first were
frequent. Did many others come to his hand after
20th March, 1793? Were the next ones likewise
intercepted? We find no trace of another letter from
Annette till the end of 1795. But one thing is sure:
that Dorothy performed without much delay her
arduous mission. She spoke to her uncle Cookson.
The result was not favourable. She complains on
16th June in a letter to her friend Jane Pollard, " of
the prejudices of her two uncles against her dear
William." [1] She must have heard a thorough indict-
ment of him, directed not only against his political
heresies, and have been somewhat shaken by it, for
she owns that " he has been somewhat to blame "; she
adds, " The subject is an unpleasant one for a letter;
it will employ us more agreeably in conversation."
But her affection will take no serious alarm. She

[1] Professor Harper's *Life of William Wordsworth*, I. p. 202.

perceives in her brother's strange and wayward nature, in his very errors, the mark of his genius.

Repulsed by his guardians, called for by Annette, what did Wordsworth do? War, which had been officially declared on 1st February, had little by little become a reality. The lovers who had, when they parted, hoped for a near reunion, found themselves divided by an almost insuperable obstacle. William could only run the risk of another journey to France at the cost of the utmost difficulties and perils. Did he run that risk? It is an open question. Much might be said to prove that he did or that he did not. On one point all his readers will be unanimous: they will wish that, for chivalry's sake, he had hastened to Annette's relief, notwithstanding his lack of money, in spite of the war and in the teeth of danger.

Against the probability of his having shown this courage there is the silence of his *Prelude* and our general knowledge of his cautious nature. His very sister had declared the year before, that he was " wise enough to get out of the way of danger." [1] A strange combination of outward circumstances and natural wariness always kept him from dangerous extravagances. Some friendly power always held him back on the brink of the precipice. He was not the man to defy fate. He it is who thought at one time of joining his destiny to that of the Girondins, but was prevented; who in the midst of the English counter-Terror wrote a proud republican letter to the Bishop of Llandaff, but kept it in manuscript and probably never even sent it to his opponent; who in 1795 wrote satirical verses against the Court and the

[1] Letter of Dorothy, 6th May, 1792. Harper II. p. 181.

Regent, but decided not to publish them. His courage was of the passive rather than of the active kind. He was capable of stubbornness and silent pertinacity, not of that fiery temper that hurls itself against the cannon's mouth.

But it is never safe to generalise. Young love may have momentarily transformed his native circumspection. There are strong reasons to believe that for once he was capable of a fine imprudence. Why did he linger for a whole month towards the end of the summer of 1793 in the Isle of Wight when nothing obliged him to do so, if he was not waiting for some smack to carry him over the Channel?[1] Besides, he must have been in France again in the autumn of 1793 if he was present at the execution of Gorsas, the first Girondin sent to the scaffold, on 7th October, as he told Carlyle in 1840.[2] If we combine this statement with an anecdote related by Alaric Watts, which evidently contains some truth and much error, Wordsworth was on this occasion alarmed by a Republican named Bailey, who told him that he would surely be guillotined if he remained in France any longer, whereupon Wordsworth fled back to England.[3] The risk he had run simply by coming

[1] I owe this suggestion to Mr. G. C. Smith, school inspector at Edinburgh, a keen Wordsworthian. On Wordsworth's feelings while he stayed in the Isle of Wight, see *Prelude*, X. 315–30.

[2] Carlyle's *Reminiscences* : see Harper's *William Wordsworth*, I. p. 209 and II. p. 417.

[3] Harper's *William Wordsworth*, I. 179. According to Watts, Bailey said: " He had met Wordsworth in Paris, and having warned him that his connection with the Mountain rendered his situation there at that time perilous, the poet decamped with great precipitation." There is no indication of time. Wordsworth could be in no danger at the end of 1792, a

D

at all, at a time of war between the two countries, was extreme. As soon as the Terror had set in, it would have been sheer madness to stay on. As a friend of the Girondins and as an Englishman he was doubly liable to suspicion.

Even if he made that bold attempt as his admirers wish it might be proved he did—as it would perhaps be proved if the family papers relating to the Annette episode had not all been destroyed—it is quite possible that he had only been able to reach Paris on his way to Blois and had had to take flight home, not only without marrying, but also without seeing Annette.

Whether he crossed the Channel or not, we know by *The Prelude* how wretched at heart he was throughout the Terror. He was shaken with anger against the ministers of his country whom he held responsible for the war; he longed for the victory of the Republic over her enemies, over the English themselves, and refused to join in the thanksgivings with which the churches of England greeted the naval successes of their people, even rejoicing within himself at the defeat of the English armies.

At first his poetry is gloomy. He puts into it all his hatred of war and takes a delight in recounting its atrocities. He paints its sinister effects on individuals and families; he gives expression to his indignation against the whole of society, which is ill-ordered, unjust, merciless to the humble, heart-

comparatively quiet period. He never was connected with the Mountain. His sympathies were all for the Girondins (Louvet against Robespierre, etc.). The anecdote is full of gross mistakes, but the fact of his being in Paris at a particularly dangerous moment, and his having decamped, can scarcely have been invented.

less and devoid of charity (*Guilt and Sorrow*). But he is, moreover, discontented with himself, conscience-stricken. In order to face needs which are no longer his only, he ought to set resolutely to work, and yet he remains the wanderer who postpones the choice of a remunerative career. He lives from hand to mouth, as unbreakable to the yoke as when he had neither burdens nor responsibilities to bear. This is the great moral fault of these years. His excuse is that, had he enriched himself by work, he could not, during the war, have shared it with wife or child. Hence a kind of inertia compounded of sundry elements: his general disgust of a society grown odious to him, his unconquerable reluctance to enter into any regular profession, his powerlessness to help the forsaken ones, and above all, the insistent call of his genius. An ordinary man would have perceived his urgent duty more clearly than the poet, harassed as he was by the demon of verse.

Besides, whilst we can be sure that he considered it his duty to help Annette, it is less certain that he remained anxious to marry her. It was in the course of this very year 1793, or very soon after, that he became the confirmed disciple of Godwin the philosopher, who was the adversary of marriage, which he proclaimed to be an evil institution, for cohabitation provided an atmosphere too dangerous and disturbing for the intellect whose supreme need was calm. The wise man would relegate marriage to its place amongst other outworn prejudices.[1] The

---

[1] The denunciation of marriage was common at that time. Charles Lloyd's novel, *Edmund Oliver* (1798), is a defence of marriage against its then numerous enemies. The story is supposed to adumbrate a passage of Coleridge's early life.

poet echoes the philosopher. He discards at that time
every institution, law, creed, rite, and only believes in

> personal Liberty,
> Which, to the blind restraints of general laws
> Superior, magisterially adopts
> One guide, the light of circumstances, flashed
> Upon an independent intellect.[1]

He may have gone further still in his enfranchisement,
and fought against pity itself, a frequent source of
injustice. Who knows but that he strove to harden
his heart like Oswald in his *Borderers*?

> The wiles of woman,
> And craft of age, seducing reason, first
> Made weakness a protection, and obscured
> The moral shapes of things.[2]

He felt that his first duty was to keep unblemished
his intellectual faculties, above all his poetic gift,
threatened by the anguished appeals from Blois.
His nature was too tender and passionate to allow
him to fortify himself against compassion. But it is
likely that he may then have tried to harden his heart
and, moreover, that he held this hardening to be a
higher virtue. His first biographer, his nephew
Bishop Wordsworth, who had in his hands and
afterwards destroyed the evidence of the case, does
not conceal that his uncle's doctrines then revealed
themselves in his very conduct. True, he attributes
the evil thereof to France and the Revolution:
" The most licentious theories were propounded, all
restraints were broken, libertinism was law." [3] Young
Wordsworth, emancipated by the Revolution, would

---

[1] *Prelude*, XI. 240-4.   [2] *The Borderers*, II. 1090-3.
[3] *Memoirs of William Wordsworth*, I. p. 74.

WILLIAM WORDSWORTH
From a drawing by Hancock in 1798

for a time appear to have resembled the solitary man of his *Excursion* who did not scruple to display " unhallowed actions . . . worn as open signs of prejudice subdued."[1] He was certainly no Don Juan, but could very well be an adept of free love.

While he was endeavouring to choke the voice of his heart and conscience by taking refuge in the abstraction of his ethical theories, Annette on the other hand, roused from her plaintive sorrow by a tragedy very near to her, was little by little infected by a political fever the violence of which was to counterpoise her love.

VIII

So grievous were the misfortunes through which the Vallons were to live during the Terror that the piteous situation of the young husbandless mother soon took a secondary place amid their troubles. Annette herself ceased to be absorbed by her own cares. At the time at which she wrote to Wordsworth and Dorothy her tearful letter, the Terror was raging at Orleans, and Paul, her favourite brother, he who had stood by her in the time of her trouble, was about to come dangerously within reach of the guillotine.

Paul Vallon found himself implicated in the alleged criminal attack on the delegate of the People— Léonard Bourdon—an affair in which ludicrous and atrocious elements are inextricably mixed. Bourdon was one of the most shameless demagogues of the

[1] *The Excursion*, II. 269–72.

Revolution, previously to which he had styled himself Bourdon de la Crosnière. The founder of an Educational Home and a clever self-advertiser, he had obtained from the *Assemblée constituante* permission to lodge in his institution the famous centenarian of the Jura, so as, he said, to impress on his pupils a respect for old age. During the *Législative*, he had managed to get himself elected as deputy for Orleans, his native town. Sent to this town in August 1792 to look into the procedure employed against the prisoners of the High Court, he had given help to Fournier, known as the American, and had in consequence taken part in that butchering of the poor wretches by the *septembrisseurs*, which we mentioned above.

Although Bourdon's complicity cannot be distinctly determined, he had acquired for himself ever since that date a criminal notoriety at Orleans. However, supported by the most turbulent elements of the town, and thanks to them sent as deputy to the Convention, he delighted in defying his opponents, the aristocrats of the national guard who were suspected of reactionary feelings.

Thus it is that in March 1793, while on a mission to the Côte d'Or, he went out of his way to see his Jacobin friends at Orleans. Without seeing any of the local authorities, he immediately presented himself amid acclamations to the People's Society, whom he excited with incendiary talk. The meeting at the club was followed by a patriotic dinner where drunkenness was added to political excitement. From the banquet-room, there soon poured forth an intoxicated and yelling mob that insulted the aristocrats on their way, and threatened the soldier

on duty at the Town Hall. The man gave the alarm,
the body of the guard rushed out and a scuffle ensued,
in which Bourdon got a few bayonet thrusts which
merely grazed his skin. The commanding officer of
the national guard was not long in liberating Bourdon.
The latter was carried to his inn and there most carefully tended. Concerned about the consequences
of the fray, the municipality expressed their regrets
to Bourdon for a fight which they could neither
foresee nor prevent.[1]

But Bourdon had made up his mind to strike the
attitude of a republican martyr. He wrote to the
Convention a letter in which he affects to be a victim
of the aristocrats. He pictures the affair as a kind
of conspiracy in which a delegate of the people
hardly escaped being murdered. He was saved, he
says, by nothing less than a miracle. If he is still
living, he owes it to a coin, now dyed with his
blood, which was in his pocket. That coin plays
the part of the blessed medal in pious stories, for
the blade, sliding along the face of the Goddess
Liberty, was only thus prevented from penetrating
more deeply.[2] Bourdon cries for revenge. At the
Convention, Barrère claims to see in the assault, the
news of which is brought by the same post as that
of the Vendée insurrection, the proof of a huge

[1] Cf. *Histoire de la Terreur*, by Mortimer Ternaux, Vol. VI.
p. 479 *et sqq.* The author is a deadly enemy of the Terrorists,
but his information is perfectly accurate, as is proved by an
examination of the original documents in the *Archives nationales*.

[2] Letter of Léonard Bourdon to the Convention of 19th
March, 1793. All the documents relating to the Bourdon
affair are found in the *Archives nationales*, BB30 87 and
AF11 167.

monarchist plot: " They want," he says, " to murder
the Republic, and begin with the patriot deputies."
Full of indignation, the Convention declare Orleans
to be in a state of rebellion, and suspend the municipal authorities. The instigators of the plot are to
be arraigned before the revolutionary court.

The mayor of Orleans, however, writes to the
Convention and asks that he may be held as sole
culprit and sole responsible person; the reading of
his generous letter instantly converts the hysterical
assembly. The sentence is repealed only to be pronounced again a few days later by the influence of
the Mountain. Not till a month later, on 26th April,
is military law to be abrogated.

During this month, Orleans lies under the terrorist
regime. Some thirty suspected persons are implicated, among whom are Wordsworth's former land-
lord, Gellet-Duvivier, and Annette's brother, Paul
Vallon.

The Jacobins at Orleans busy themselves in gather-
ing evidence against the aristocrats and the national
guard, which they hate. One of them, who was also
one of the most active supporters of Bourdon, the
apothecary Besserve, writes to his good brothers and
friends to assure them that the affair is being actively
followed up, that the accused have grounds for some
uneasiness, that his own evidence has terrified more
than one of them, that he spoke with the frankness
characteristic of the genuine republican and honest
man, and that " he showed Truth so naked that
more than one judge fell in love with her." [1]

[1] Tuetey, *Répertoire général des Sources manuscrites de
l'histoire de Paris pendant la Révolution française*, Vol. VIII
p. 278.

One can with difficulty form an idea of the idleness of most of the charges gathered by the delegates of the executive power who held the inquiry at Orleans. There may be some truth as regards poor Gellet-Duvivier. Not being fully responsible for his actions, he had shown extreme excitement in the scuffle amongst the national guard, in which he was a grenadier. Not only did he hurl insults against Bourdon and the Convention, but he took the deputy by the throat, knocked him down and struck him with his sword. It is even said that he fired one shot. Thus he was the first to be arrested.

But one reads with bewilderment the charges brought against Paul Vallon, who was on special duty at the Town Hall.

Citizen " X " gives evidence that a young citizen [told him] that having seized by the throat a young man who uttered insolent words and insulted Bourdon and the patriots, the young man thus seized cried out that he was not the man, and that citizen Vallon used every means to tear himself out of the hands of the patriots who held him.

Citizen " Y " gives evidence that being at the Place de l'Étape, he heard three or four young men who were gunners, grenadiers or chasseurs, say on seeing the patriots drawing near, " Here come the knave Goullu, the rascal Besserve and the other scoundrels "; that in the same moment there came out of the courtyard of the municipal buildings some thirty young men, that three of four of the said young men surrounded the witness, that one of them called at the top of his voice for one Vallon; and, seeing the said Vallon did not come, they turned back to assault citizen Besserve.[1]

[1] *Archives nationales*, AF[11] 167, No. 137.

Paul Vallon had tried to disengage himself from
the patriots' hands; he had *not* come to the assaulters'
help, but had been called to the rescue by one of
them, and this evidence was amply sufficient to lose
him his head. Was he not known in town as a friend
of the old regime?

Yet some hope dawned for the accused. Other
representatives of the people passing through Orleans,
gave an account to the Convention of the wretched
state of the town (11th May); by their statements
the criminal attempt was reduced to a mere scuffle,
the responsibility of which was thrown on to Bourdon.
On 19th May, Noël read a report exonerating the
town council and incriminating Bourdon.   The
Mountain grew indignant. The Girondin Louvet
made an eloquent reply. The Convention followed
Noel's lead and cancelled their former verdict. But
a fortnight later, the Mountain had the upper
hand again.   The accused, transferred to Paris,
to the Conciergerie du Palais, were arraigned by
Fouquier-Tinville before his tribunal.

Gellet-Duvivier's daughter—a minor—now presented a petition, in which she explains that since
his wife's death her poor father's mind is unhinged,
that the people of Orleans know him to be weak-
minded, that since his arrest his madness has become
complete, that his incoherent shouting prevents his
fellow-prisoners from sleeping, that when she visits
her father, he does not recognise her, calls her his
wife and offers to marry her. She demands for him
a medical examination so that his madness or weak-
mindedness may be certified.

In correct style, Fouquier-Tinville granted the
examination, but poor Gellet-Duvivier nevertheless

was one of the nine accused from Orleans to mount the scaffold on 13th July.

Nearly two years passed after 9th Thermidor before the iniquitous case was revised. Six sections of the commune of Dijon—the town Bourdon visited just after the scuffle at Orleans—then denounced the deputy as having boasted that he had himself purposely provoked the fray (9th May, 1795). Bourdon, who, in the meantime, had had his period of grandeur, who had succeeded to Robespierre as president of the Jacobins, who had dared to stand up against him—not indeed as a moderating factor but by virtue of his alliance with the Hébertists or *Enragés* (maddened ones)—and who, urged by his fear of his powerful enemy, had helped to accomplish his overthrow—Bourdon was denounced as " infamous " by his colleagues, though they had been witnesses to many kinds of inhumanity. Legendre, during a séance of the Convention, Boissy d'Anglas in the Council of the Five Hundred, one after the other called him murderer. He lasted out till the Empire, however, having returned to his educational calling and become head of a primary school.

Meanwhile, more cautious or more lucky than Gellet-Duvivier, Paul Vallon succeeded in saving his head. When they tried to arrest him on 24th April, 1793, he had disappeared. He figures among the accused, marked down as absent, whom Fouquier-Tinville indicted on 16th June, and ordered to be committed to the Conciergerie. He was in hiding at Orleans at the house of a M. Lochon-Petitbois, a merchant and a friend of the family.[1]

[1] Manuscript memoirs of Amédée Vallon, Paul's son.

But we may well imagine the anxiety of his friends, and of his sisters, during all these months when the least word might cause his death. No doubt he was assisted by them as far as lay in their power, with the constant fear of their very help betraying him. No doubt also that the atrocious injustice under which their brother laboured inspired these women with the hatred of the Revolution.

This miserable affair must have occupied a great part of the letters which Annette continued to send Wordsworth. But did he get them? And did his own letters reach her? The first he received, as far as we know, is that of which Dorothy speaks to a friend in November 1795: "William has had a letter from France since we came here. Annette mentions having despatched half a dozen, none of which he has received." [1] The violence of the war rendered all correspondence precarious, if not impossible. However, relations became frequent again during the preliminaries of the Peace of Amiens. Then from 21st December, 1801, to 24th March, 1802, are noted down in Dorothy's diary a series of letters exchanged between the poet and Annette. It is clear that their correspondence was as active as possible, and that circumstances alone prevented it from being carried on continuously.

[1] Letter of Dorothy to Mrs. Marshall of 30th November, 1795. See Harper, I. p. 292.

IX

IF, in this new series of letters, Annette has no such tragic adventures to relate, yet misfortunes and dangers have not ceased to beset her and her friends after a short period of calm.

The Terror once over, Paul Vallon having come out of his hiding-place and returned to the office of Maître Courtois, it seems there was a short period during which the Vallon family could breathe in peace. The three sisters lived together at Blois, poorly enough no doubt (but who was not poor then?), but on good terms with the best society of the town. They lived with their mother and stepfather at the family house in the Rue du Pont. Sheltered by the name of Madame William that she had assumed, or of Veuve William—for one finds both in turn—Annette, protected from scandal, was bringing up Caroline. Her brother Charles Henry, who had become head of the family at the death of Jean Jacques, was in a prosperous situation as head surgeon at the Hospital of Blois.

Life, after the fall of Robespierre and throughout the Directory, in spite of persisting troubles, in spite of war and the general impoverishment of the country, had the sweetness of convalescence. It seems to have had at Blois a peculiar charm, according to Dufort, Comte de Cheverny, who drew in his *Memoirs* this idyllic picture:

Thanks be rendered to the inhabitants of the town of Blois, who have succeeded in making of the society which gather there the pleasantest that may be imagined. Blois is in every way preferable to its three neighbours,

Orleans, Vendôme and Tours, a distinction it has always enjoyed. The general lack of means has levelled all rivalry and there is no disparity in rank. The insignificant trade that is being carried on does not arouse competition. The few people who live at Blois stay by reason of its irresistible attraction. . . . Despite [he adds] the poverty suffered by all classes, there are gatherings of twenty, thirty people, sometimes more. The stranger admitted to these parties might think himself in the midst of a family. Women are elegantly dressed, and there are numbers of marriageable young girls, every one prettier than the next. Music is carried to a point of great perfection. [They give concerts] that would be deemed good even in Paris.[1]

A fine spirit of generosity prevailed towards the victims of the Revolution, according to another witness, the wife of Doctor Chambon de Montaux, who lived at Blois from 1793 to 1804:

One would never end if one tried to give an account of the acts of kindness performed by the people of Blois on behalf of the unhappy proscribed. We were welcomed and helped as brothers by the nobility of the town—true to king and state. Our tears were dried by the hand of friendship.[2]

Royalists were numerous and active. Blois was "one of the most ardent centres of the counter-revolution." The 9th of Thermidor raised great hopes. The Vendémiaire insurrection found in Blois zealous agents who corresponded with the Paris sections in

[1] *Mémoires sur les Règnes de Louis XV. et Louis XVI. et sur la Révolution*, par J. N. Dufort, Comte de Cheverny, Introducteur des Ambassadeurs, Lieutenant Général du Blaisois (1732–1802), publiées par Robert de Crèvecœur. Tome II.

[2] Quoted in *Mémoires de Madame Vallon*, published by Guy Trouillard, p. 223 (note).

revolt, and among these agents men such as Guyon de Montlivault and Pardessus the younger, to whom we constantly find reference among the friends of the Vallon sisters. These early hopes were to be wrecked on 13th Vendémiaire (5th October, 1795) by young Bonaparte on the steps of the church of St. Roch. At first great discouragement ensued for the royalists. The tone of Annette's letter mentioned by Dorothy on 30th November, must have been very different according as it was written before or after 13th Vendémiaire.

But soon the party took heart again. Without renouncing their aim, they changed their tactics. To the Parisian insurrection succeeded the provincial *chouannerie* of which Blois was to be one of the chief centres and into which Annette threw herself heart and soul. She allied herself with the most combative among the Chouans, those criticised by the Comte de Cheverny, whose own ideal was to keep himself and family safe by "an absolute nullity." [1]

Cheverny is full of recriminations against the imprudent members of his class or party, whose intrigues endanger the security of others. Yet when the occasion comes, when a clever stroke has been well struck, he is fain to applaud it. Thus he relates with relish a certain incident at Blois in which one of the three sisters bears a part.

It occurred after an anti-royalist move on the part of the Directory. The act of the 22nd of Germinal, in the fourth year of the Republic (11th April, 1796), had just prescribed new penalties against non-juring priests and emigrants. There happened to be **two**

[1] *Mémoires de Cheverny*, II. p. 128.

emigrants in the prison of Blois. A plot was formed in the town to help them to escape. One morning five persons were arrested before the prison by a patrol; among them was Lacaille the younger, aged sixteen years, gunsmith, and surgeon's apprentice under Vallon. They were accused of having planned the escape of the emigrants. On the ground by them was found a very well-made rope-ladder. And Cheverny adds here:

A *demoiselle* Vallon, of meritorious character and of an obliging disposition, is questioned by the jury as to having ordered twenty-seven fathoms of rope to make the ladder which was to save the prisoners. She owns to having ordered the rope but says it is still in her attic, which is proved true. Thus she is pronounced not guilty.[1]

If Cheverny congratulates her, it is probably because he thinks she showed both daring in abetting the escape and skill in getting out of the difficulty. He rejoices at the happy issue of the case which, in compliance with the request of the accused, had been tried in Orleans. Once acquitted, they came back triumphantly to Blois in the carriage of Brunet the coffee-house keeper, and a scuffle ensued between their followers and the Jacobin post on duty, in which the latter got the worst of it.

Although we cannot say for certain which of the Vallon sisters Cheverny has in mind, there are many reasons to believe that it was Annette, who is always noted as the most active of the trio. She now definitely separated herself from her uncles, the constitutional priests, and went back to the old form of worship. Her signature is found to a secret Roman

[1] *Mémoires de Cheverny*, II. p. 295.

Catholic marriage, held in the private chapel used instead of the parish church of St. Honoré, on 14th July, 1795. This is the one and only time she signs herself William Wordsworth Vallon. It seems that her enthusiasm carried away her relations. On 29th December, 1796, her brother Charles Henry, who two years earlier had contracted a civil marriage with a girl named Charruyau, had their union secretly consecrated by a non-juring priest in a room of the house in the Rue Pierre de Blois, used instead of the church of St. Solenne.[1]

Annette and her sisters, but more particularly Annette, were allied to those too energetic families who fell under the displeasure of Cheverny. They were at the very heart of that *chouannerie* whose leaders were such men as Pardessus the younger, Charles de Rancogne, Guyon de Montlivault, with whom they were closely acquainted.

Guyon de Montlivault was the nominal head of the Blois *chouannerie*. Cheverny, who disliked him for his turbulence, speaks of him as ambitious and trusted by nobody. Montlivault certainly lacked circumspection. He ingenuously betrayed the secrets of the conspiracy to a spy who passed himself off on him as a Chouan and who, on 3rd March, 1797, sent a report on the councils of the Chouans to the Ministry of Police: " I learned through him," says the spy, " that Blois had a paid Chouan brigade, bound by the customary oath, recruited among the artisans and labourers, but of established moral character and formed only to ensure the secret execution of the Council's designs." Their

[1] Notes furnished by Abbé J. Gallerand, professor at the Seminary of Blois.

E

procedure was to provoke the former Terrorists to make trouble so that the suspicions of the Directory might be shifted on to them. The Chouans were under oath to render every assistance to the Catholic and royal party.[1]

It was no mere affair of caste, as may be seen. The bulk of the soldiery was drawn from the people. Part of the population lightheartedly entered the fight against the Jacobins, insulted and reviled them, occasionally came to blows with them. In the ranks of the conspirators were found men of all ranks. The Vallon sisters threw their house open to noblemen such as Montlivault and Rancogne, to *bourgeois* such as Jean Marie Pardessus, to artisans such as the gunsmith Lacaille and his sons, to mention only those whose names are coupled with theirs in the police reports. Pardessus's father had been in custody during the Terror, his younger brother was killed at Savenay, fighting under Larochejaquelin, Jean Marie himself was the ordinary counsel for the Chouans of the region when brought to justice. Charles, the son of the Marquis de Rancogne, despite the entreaties of his father—as timorous as Cheverny himself—was for a time a captain under Georges Cadoudal. The younger Lacaille too, it is said, fought under the same chief. Lacaille's very apprentices were known for their extremist opinions; one of them was later shot at Brest under suspicion of espionage in English pay.

The usual meeting-place of the Chouans was, doubtless, Berruet's coffee-house, " The Three

---

[1] Mémoires sur les Conseils Chouans remis au Ministre de la Police générale le 13 Ventôse an V. (3 mars, 1797): Archives nationales, F7 6200.

Merchants." But there were more secret haunts, used chiefly by those who were being tracked down, and the house of the Vallon sisters was one of these shelters. We do not know the name of those " numberless " French people who, as we are told by a Restoration document,[1] owed their salvation to Annette, of those who were " saved, hidden and assisted by her," of the persecuted emigrants and priests whom she helped to escape from prison and death. Among those who later testify to her devotedness, only one, the Chevalier de la Rochemouhet, declares that " Madame William saved his life at the peril of her own." The others are witnesses to her devotion rather than personally her debtors: Théodore de Montlivault, the Comte de Salaberry, the Vicomte de Malartic, the Baron de Tardif, etc. . . . It is just possible that the Vicomte de Montmorency-Laval owed her some direct assistance in his troubles. Formerly a staunch liberal—he had gone as far as to move, on the night of 4th August, the abolition of the aristocratic privileges — he had repented of what he termed his errors; towards the end of the century he was in the department of Loir-et-Cher under threat of arrest. When the Bourbons came back to the throne, he gave proof of his gratitude to Annette.

All those who struck at the Jacobins won Annette's sympathy, amongst others Nicolas Bailly, whom we shall meet later as her great friend. It was he who, entrusted with the public prosecutor's speech against Babeuf and his followers at Vendôme in May 1797, contributed to the condemnation of the redoubtable socialist and to the fall of his Jacobin supporters.

[1] See Appendix IV.

The activity of the Vallon sisters, and chiefly of
Annette, was extreme and could not long escape the
attention of the government. The police searches
ranged nearer and nearer and ended in the compila-
tion of a long list of suspected persons, whose
arrest was decreed by the Minister of Justice. This
vigilance began at the end of the Directory, and
continued into the first months of the Consulate.
From 10th October, 1799, to 31st January, 1800,
were indicted: Montlivault, Montmorency-Laval,
Rancogne the younger, Jean Marie Pardessus, Puzéla
(Paul Vallon's future father-in-law, whom we shall
meet again), among many others. Annette was one of
the persons *not* to be arrested on the spot, but for
whom "it were advisable to have an order for a
domiciliary search to examine their papers and arrest
them if any plotting is discovered" (police document,
31st January, 1800). She is marked down on the
police paper as "Widow Williams at Blois; gives
shelter to the Chouans." [1]

We do not know whether the search took place.
It is certain, however, that more coherent action
was being taken against the Chouans. Most of them
were discovered; some were imprisoned, others
placed under supervision and rendered powerless.
The big fight in the West ended on 26th January,
1800, with Georges Cadoudal's defeat at Pont de
Loch, followed by his submission. The Chouans
were capable of nothing more than spasmodic
movements in the following years.

This was a source of sadness for a zealous royalist
like Annette, and personal troubles were added to it.
Her eldest sister Françoise, at more than thirty-

[1] Archives nationales, F7 6200.

five years old, was implicated in a mysterious and painful adventure.

We must imagine the strange atmosphere in which these women conspirators moved in order to understand—there is no question of excusing—what happened to Françoise. We must consider the perturbing promiscuity of excited men and women maddened in turn with anger and with fear, the secret meetings, the long whisperings, the feverish intimacy, when pity provokes love and danger leads to unrestraint. In 1798, Françoise gave birth to a son whose father is not known. Given the extraordinary laxity of morals throughout the country during the Directory, the mad thirst for pleasure which carried away all classes, and the general discredit into which marriage had fallen, this might have been a simple occurrence enough at a time when so many men and women " followed nature." But in the house of the Vallon sisters, who were known for their devotion to Church and Throne, and who were nieces of two priests, the matter was different. It was a scandal in the very sanctuary. What jeers, what sarcasms would be levelled at the Catholic conspirators! How their adversaries would make use of the adventure to ridicule the Cause itself! Thus Françoise was induced, after having concealed her state, to abandon the child. The very day of its birth (1st November, 1798), it was exposed at the Hospital of Blois, where, on account of the date (11th Brumaire of the seventh year of the Republic), they gave it the names of Toussaint Décadi. Both calendars were thus united: Décadi, a revolutionary name, striking a strangely false note in the records of a monarchist family.

We must remember that Françoise's brother, Charles

Henry, was head of the hospital. We may conclude that he connived at the plan and exercised special supervision over the disowned child. Nature had been sacrificed to the Cause, but it would be wrong to regard Françoise as devoid of all maternal feeling. She suffered and did not forget. Twenty years later, when settled away from Blois, in Paris, where she was safe from the malicious curiosity of neighbours, she owned Toussaint Décadi as her child (22nd May, 1819), and some time afterwards married him to a girl of illegitimate birth, who could not upbraid him with his own (22nd July, 1820).

At the same time, Annette was beset with other anxieties concerning her brother Paul, who suddenly left Orleans, in 1800, to lead in Paris a precarious and disorderly existence of which we shall speak further.

It is not probable that Annette related all these misfortunes in the letters received from her by Wordsworth at the beginning of 1802, but she could tell enough to justify Dorothy's exclamation, "Poor Annette!"

X

WHILE these various cares engrossed Annette and severed from him, if not her heart, at least her thoughts, the poet himself was drifting from the love that had long possessed him by turns with delight and with suffering. We can ascribe to the end of 1795 the growing estrangement of which at first he may not have been quite conscious. During the Terror, his passion had been kept on the alert by

the dread of the scaffold to which he might think
Annette exposed, realising as he did her generous
imprudence. He has related the nightmares that
haunted his sleep, without confessing, however, that
they were not merely called up by vague and general
fears, but by intimate and tangible realities. There
was, moreover, no abatement in his love for France.
He saw the crimes that were committed, but he also
saw the acts of heroism which shone through that
darkness. He deplored the actions of the ruling
party, but preserved his faith in the people " and in
the virtues which his eyes had seen." [1] Circumstances
had simultaneously brought into existence his love
for the woman who was becoming an ardent
royalist and his enthusiasm for republican France.
The destinies of these two passions remained strangely
interwoven. As long as France continued to be
the land on which his hopes centred, Annette had
no reason to fear forgetfulness or estrangement.

But the war continued, still preventing the wished-
for meeting. By slow degrees, France, becoming a
warlike nation, lost her prestige for him—France,
together with all he had left there. The indefinite
duration of hostilities obliged him to fix his life in
his own country since he was shut out from the other.
His need of feminine tenderness was almost satisfied
by his re-union with his sister Dorothy, in whom
he discovered treasures of imaginative and poetical
sympathy of which his French friend, unacquainted
with his tongue, deaf to his verses, unaccustomed to
rural life, was quite incapable. Besides, a prolonged
feeling of powerlessness brings with it a kind of
paralysis of the affections. Had he been willing to

[1] *Prelude*, XI. 87.

atone for the harm done to Annette, he could not
have done so. Had he been desirous of helping her
in the accomplishment of her maternal duty, he had
neither the money nor the means of sending it.

When, by his friend Raisley Calvert's legacy in
1795, he was enabled to dispose of £900, he could
not use this sum in assisting mother and child. He
used it as is well known. He secured for himself out
of the income of his modest capital a very frugal
life devoted to poetry, which he shared with his
sister at Racedown. And the happiness he enjoyed
there was such that after a time he must have felt
a secret terror of any alteration in his mode of living
that would deprive him of Dorothy, tear him from
the Muse and the country. When to Dorothy was
added Coleridge, when his emotional and intellectual life was in a way complete, when the first poems
which gave him the certainty of his genius gushed
out, and he advanced towards the composition of
the *Lyrical Ballads* in the combined joy of friendship and poetry; above all, when from the confusion
in which Godwin's anarchic doctrines had left him,
he turned again to his own country, which day after
day became dearer and more indispensable to his
heart, and steeped himself again in the remotest
memories of his childhood centred round the Lake
district—then the thought of Annette and Caroline,
moving as it still was, no longer came before his
eyes save as a troubling vision, contrary to the
direction now followed by the flow of his existence.

There was not, at first, any lessening of his sympathy for their distress nor of the feeling of the
obligations he had incurred. But when troubled by
his recollections, he used the famous Goethean re-

cipe and turned his memories into verse. His poetry in these years teems with subjects in which his own distress is poured forth, in dramatic form, in affecting stories of seduced maidens, forsaken wives, or simply of wretched women whose lives have been wrecked by the war. Sometimes the details of the story are widely different from Annette's, sometimes they closely resemble it, but in all these tales— the recurrence of which might justly astonish us if we knew nothing of his own adventure—we find the same pathos issuing from a heart tormented by remembrance and remorse.

Thus, in *The Ruined Cottage* [1] (1797), or the tale of Margaret, we have the story of a woman happy before war spreads desolation over the country, whose husband one day joins the colours, driven thereto by unemployment, and never comes back. She sees her little child die, her garden grow waste, her cottage fall to ruins.

In *The Thorn* (1798), we are given the sad picture of Martha Ray, forsaken and left with child by Stephen Hill, who marries another. She kills her infant and becomes half mad with grief and remorse. She constantly returns to weep on the mound planted with a thorn, where the villagers think she buried the little corpse.

Above all, in *Her eyes are wild* (1798), one of his most moving ballads, we hear the lament of the poor woman deserted by her husband while she suckles her babe—a prolonged complaint, a poignant appeal to the forgetful absent one. Had not the poet the frequent vision of another forsaken woman

[1] Afterwards inserted by him in the First Book of *The Excursion*.

lulling her babe to rest, who could indeed imagine, as she looked in vain for the return of the father, that he no longer cared for her? Here we distinctly recognise some of the feelings to which Annette gives expression in her letter of 1793:[1]

> Thy father cares not for my breast,
> 'Tis thine, sweet baby, there to rest;
> 'Tis all thine own!—and if its hue
> Be changed, that was so fair to view,
> 'Tis fair enough for thee, my dove!
> My beauty, little child, is flown,
> But thou wilt live with me in love;
> And what if my poor cheek be brown?
> 'Tis well for me thou canst not see
> How pale and wan it else would be.
>
> Dread not their taunts, my little Life;
> I am thy father's wedded wife:
> And underneath the spreading tree
> We two will live in honesty.
> If his sweet boy he could forsake,

[1] *Cf.* in Annette's letter: " She is such a pretty little one, so pretty that my love of her almost distracts me unless I hold her continually in my arms. . . . Behold your wife; sorrow has altered her much. Do you know her? . . . If her features are altered . . . her heart is unchanged. It is still yours. Know your Annette, Caroline's tender mother." . . . " I cannot express the degree of my love for my daughter. When I hold her in my arms I often repeat to her: ' Caroline, my dear child, you have not your father; he is far away, poor little one. . . . Call him to you, my pet. . . .'—The only pleasure left me is to see her. . . . ' Your father is not so happy as I, Caroline, he will not see you with this tiny cap on your head.' "

Wordsworth never read that letter, but he received many others which perhaps came much nearer the feelings expressed in his ballad.

With me he never would have stayed:
From him no harm my babe can take;
But he, poor man, is wretched made;
And every day we two will pray
For him that's gone and far away.

Again there is *Ruth* (1799), who is carried away by the sweet words of the young Georgian, by his enchanting descriptions of the Tropics. She allows him to lead her to the altar, but the young husband, soon caught again by his passion for a free and wandering life, shortly after leaves her and she becomes mad with grief.

Fifteen years later, we find the same story told again in *The Excursion*,[1] but this time in a tone of edification. We are invited to mourn over the poor young peasant girl Ellen, so grave and so beautiful, who yet was seduced and had for sole comfort the child of her sin. Poverty drives her to hire herself as a nurse; her child dies. Ellen fades away and dies full of repentance.

XI

THUS did Wordsworth give utterance to his trouble when he thought of Annette. This is certainly not forgetfulness. In letters he wrote to Dorothy in 1800 he still spoke with tender feeling of Annette and her child. But what was beyond his control was to prevent his imagination from becoming estranged from her as from a being alien to his deeper nature. She appeared to him more and more as an accident, a surprise in the course of his existence. As early

[1] Book VI. 786–1073.

as 1799, he had repudiated her poetically, had out of
the secrecy of his past discovered a favoured rival.
He had sacrificed her to the memory of Lucy.

The Lucy poems, which are among the purest
jewels of the Wordsworthian poetry, were written
during a stay he made at Goslar, in Germany, with
Dorothy, in 1799. Read in the light of Annette's
adventure, they assume a newer and perhaps a
deeper meaning.

Doubtless she remains an enigma to us, this young
Lucy, to whose cottage the poet went on horseback
in the moonlight. We have here the memory of a
youthful love which it is fit we should place before
that for Annette. It is indeed at this date—1799—
that Wordsworth's mind reverts to the early time of
his life and to his native hills, in order to draw new
faith and strength from them. One can fancy Lucy
loved by the Hawkshead pupil about the end of his
school time, or by the Cambridge student during
one of his vacations. What we have to consider here
is that Wordsworth conveys to her, into the grave
where she has long been buried, the assurance that
it is she whom he was right in loving, she whose
love had sunk deepest into his heart.

She had indeed two claims on his love, over which
nothing now seems to him able to prevail. She was
a mountain girl, dwelling in a secluded and lovely
dale. Nature meant to mould her herself, to make
of her " a lady of her own." Her beauty was like
the reflection of the beauty of heaven, of clouds,
springs and woods:

> And hers shall be the breathing balm,
> And hers the silence and the calm
> Of mute insensate things.

The floating clouds their state shall lend
To her; for her the willow bend;
Nor shall she fail to see
Even in the motions of the Storm
Grace that shall mould the Maiden's form
By silent sympathy.

The stars of midnight shall be dear
To her; and she shall lean her ear
In many a secret place
Where rivulets dance their wayward round,
And beauty born of murmuring sound
Shall pass into her face.

Lucy's other claim was that she was English. No
doubt it is the weariness of his stay in Germany,
which forces from the poet a vow nevermore to
leave his country. No doubt his time in France had
been very different and he had then rebelled against
the necessity which recalled him to London. But now
all foreign countries are repellent to him. He recon-
ciles himself with his own country over Lucy's grave:

I travelled among unknown men,
    In lands beyond the sea;
Nor, England! did I know till then
    What love I bore to thee.

'Tis past, that melancholy dream!
    Nor will I quit thy shore
A second time; for still I seem
    To love thee more and more.

Among thy mountains did I feel
    The joy of my desire;
And she I cherished turned her wheel
    Beside an English fire.

Thy mornings showed, thy nights concealed,
    The bowers where Lucy played;
And thine too is the last green field
    That Lucy's eyes surveyed.

It may be that these verses were not directed against Annette, but they pass her over and, by ignoring her, they pronounce her doom. *She* it is who owes nothing to the soil or sky of England, who speaks another language, who would be an exile in an English village and wondered at by the villagers. Above all she is town-born and town-bred, garrulous of speech and possessed of all the worldly qualities which the poet now proclaims worthless if not reprehensible, and there are in her none of the inclinations that bind a soul to Nature. She is a foreigner and a townswoman. If ever the poet now did marry her, it would be out of gratitude or from a sense of duty, but with the inward certainty of having wrecked his life.

XII

Now, thanks to his sister, he finds the new Lucy in so far as it is possible for another woman to renew the miracle of an apparition beloved at the dawn of youth, and made divine by death. He had quite forgotten her, that Mary Hutchinson who was his schoolfellow at the Penrith dame's school, and whom he had seen again, with pleasure, in the same place during his summer holidays of 1789. In later years she had long been driven from his thoughts by Annette. Dorothy herself, who was her comrade, had neglected her for her bosom friend Miss Pollard. But Miss Pollard was now married, and time, distance and silence had caused Annette's memory to fade more and more. Dorothy, in whom every other consideration gave way to the duty of protecting her brother's genius, invited Mary to visit her at Racedown, where she spent the spring of 1797, not seeing much of the poet however, who frequently absented himself during this time. It is after the journey to Germany and the Lucy poems that William appears to have been convinced that the happiness of his life would be found in a marriage with the gentle and quiet English girl, who knew and loved rustic life so well. In May 1800, he went to see her at the Yorkshire farm where she and her family lived, and in her turn she spent the winter of 1801–2 at Dove Cottage, the humble house at Grasmere, in the Lake Country, in which Wordsworth and Dorothy had settled at the beginning of the century. Meanwhile, the poet addressed to Mary a definite declaration of love, for what other name can we give to the poem to Mary Hutchinson written and published as early as 1800? [1]

In a walk amid the woods he found a delightful secluded glade, enclosing a lawn and a small pool. The place was sheltered from the hot sun and the rough wind. This peaceful retreat immediately blended itself in his mind with the soothing image of Mary. It is unknown to travellers:

> . . . but it is beautiful;
> And if a man should plant his cottage near,
> Should sleep beneath the shelter of its trees,
> And blend its waters with his daily meal,
> He would so love it, that in his death-hour
> Its image would survive among his thoughts:
> And therefore, my sweet Mary, this still Nook,
> With all its beeches, we have named from You.

[1] *To M. H.:* " Our walk was far . . ."

The declaration was made, and if anything still withheld Wordsworth from marrying, it was not Annette, but his lack of money, or rather, it seems, his inability to support both Annette and Mary: was he not to provide for his daughter's education? (He had decidedly abandoned the thought of making Annette his wife.) He also had—and here his courage is seen—to tell Mary everything, if he had not done so before. It is true that this confession was then less difficult than it seemed to be a generation later. A natural child was a frequent occurrence and did not mean so much.[1] Whatever else we may think, Wordsworth's honesty is evident. To him the lot of the two women was interdependent. He wished neither Mary to be ignorant of his past nor Annette of his decision. We read in Dorothy's diary of 31st March, 1802:

A rainy day. William very poorly. Two letters from Sarah [Mary's sister] and one from poor Annette. . . . We resolved to see Annette, and that William should go to Mary.

The pecuniary condition was fulfilled almost immediately after this decision. In June, Wordsworth learned that the son of the old Earl of Lonsdale who had just died, would pay his father's debt; and Mary was told without delay. Dorothy and he were to leave Grasmere to go and see her. From now on she was his betrothed.

This is proved by the *Farewell* he addressed, before leaving his little Dove Cottage, to his garden and flowers, promising them a speedy return with her who is to be his wife:

[1] See *ante*, p. 4.

We go for One to whom ye will be dear;
And she will prize this Bower, this Indian shed,
Our own contrivance, Building without peer!
—A gentle Maid, whose heart is lowly bred,
Whose pleasures are in wild fields gathered,
With joyousness, and with a thoughtful cheer,
Will come to you; to you herself will wed;
And love the blessed life that we lead here. . . .

O happy Garden! . . .
Two burning months let summer overleap,
And, coming back with Her who will be ours,
Into thy bosom we again shall creep.

Brother and sister start for Gallow Hill, near Scar-
borough, where they spend ten days near Mary,
from 16th to 26th July. Then by way of London
they reach Calais, where Annette had agreed to
meet them, arriving there on 1st August. They
stayed four weeks with her and Caroline.

XIII

ALTHOUGH we can fairly well guess the reasons for
the visit, there is still something strange about this
August spent at Calais with Annette. Their correspondence had been resumed as soon as the preliminaries of peace made it possible. Wordsworth
was to go to her as soon as the treaty of Amiens
opened France again to him. This alacrity might
well induce one to think his passion was still alive.
No doubt, by taking his sister along with him,
Wordsworth plainly meant that there was no question
of a renewal of their former irregular relations.
Dorothy was, so to speak, acting as a chaperon.
But to consecrate four weeks to the parting of two

F

lovers is a somewhat extraordinary proceeding, especially when one considers that during that time Mary was awaiting her lover.

Everything seems to have passed simply and cordially, without transports of affection or outbursts of passion. In Dorothy's diary of the period, written just after her return to Grasmere, we read:

We found Annette and Caroline *chez Madame Avril dans la rue de la Tête d'Or*. . . . We walked by the seashore almost every evening with Annette and Caroline or William and I alone. One night I shall never forget—the day had been very hot, and William and I walked alone together upon the pier.—

" Alone," that is without Annette, for Dorothy adds: " Caroline was delighted."

It was on this occasion that Wordsworth wrote one of his most famous sonnets, the only one of his poems that relates to his French daughter:

It is a beauteous evening, calm and free;
The holy time is quiet as a Nun
Breathless with adoration; the broad sun
Is sinking down in its tranquillity;
The gentleness of heaven broods o'er the Sea:
Listen! the mighty Being is awake,
And doth with his eternal motion make
A sound like thunder—everlastingly.
Dear Child! dear Girl! that walkest with me here,
If thou appear untouched by solemn thought,
Thy nature is not therefore less divine:
Thou liest in Abraham's bosom all the year;
And worshipp'st at the Temple's inner shrine,
God being with thee when we know it not.

There is certainly nothing in this pious effusion, full of biblical and religious evocations, to betray the presence of a natural daughter of the poet. That is why many critics have thought that Wordsworth here addressed his own sister—regardless of the fact that Dorothy was of all women the most exquisitely sensitive to natural beauty. To us who are better informed, this almost sacerdotal blessing offers a striking example of the way in which Wordsworth was apt to solemnise the most mundane passages of his life. It may either irritate or amuse readers averse from all untimely and inopportune solemnity. There is indeed a wonderful forgetfulness of contingencies, a rare lack of compunction in the father, a frail sinner, who transforms himself into a sovereign pontiff.

But the words in the sonnet which are of greatest import to us are " untouched by solemn thought," which furnish us with a key to the imaginative disagreement between the Wordsworths and not only Caroline, but also—and still more—Annette. To be sure Caroline was a ten-year-old child who was readier to play on Calais pier than to contemplate with august emotion the setting of the sun in the sea. All we know of her tends to prove that she was playful and lively, more sociable than contemplative. It is no mere question of age. Annette, like her daughter, was ill-fitted for prolonged ecstasies in the presence of nature. Her mind would soon turn back to her ordinary cares, to her friends at Blois, to the political intrigues she had left in suspense to revisit her former lover.

William and she had now only one common feeling, their hatred of Bonaparte; and even in this they differed, for they hated him for diametrically opposite reasons. Annette execrated in him the hero of 13th Vendémiaire who had ruined the last royalist hopes, the Consul who, instead of using his absolute power to restore the Bourbons, was stifling *chouannerie* and preparing the accession of his own dynasty. Precisely on the 15th of that month of August, fell the anniversary of his birth and the proclamation of his Consulship for life. They were sources of common woe and indignation for the two lovers of yore. But Wordsworth's anger was roused by seeing his republican dreams belied and set at naught by the return of tyranny. He was exasperated with those of his compatriots who were pouring into France to salute the new despot. He contrasted the Calais of 1802 with that of 1790, the official and joyless pomps of the present festivities with the raptures of true mirth at the Federation. The words " Good morrow, citizen," which had made his heart beat faster and had seemed to him the very accents of fraternity, were now, though he still heard them here and there, " a hollow word, as if a dead man spoke it." [1]

His rekindling patriotism was fanned by the disappointment caused by this new visit to the country in which he had once so nearly lost it. What a change! The English name was no longer on French soil, as it was wont to be, a token of honour, a symbol of Freedom; it was an enemy's name, frequently coupled with curses. War had filled the souls of the two peoples with mutual hatred. He felt the weakness of the peace treaty which had enabled him to make this journey:

> I, with many a fear
> For my dear Country, many heartfelt sighs,
> Among men who do not love her, linger here. [2]

[1] Sonnet: " Jones! as from Calais . . ."
[2] Sonnet: " Fair Star of evening . . ."

All the acts, past or present, of the new master were hateful to him. As a poet he lamented the extinction of the Venetian Republic,[1] so great in the memories of men. He pitied Toussaint L'Ouverture who was thrown into prison.[2] He waxed indignant at the return to slavery decreed in the very country in which all men had so recently been proclaimed free. He execrated the act which drove all the negroes from France.[3]

However, he did not yet recant his old affection for France. He did not yet decisively take sides with either of the two nations which—in this time of peace —were moving towards an imminent and terrible encounter. He tried to divert his thoughts from the present so that he might cling to hope:

> Happy is he, who caring not for Pope,
> Consul, or King, can sound himself to know
> The destiny of Man, and live in hope.

With his mind thus engaged, feeling himself already half a stranger, he listened with inattentive ears to the long tales recounted by Annette of the politics of Blois, of the conspiracies into which she had ardently plunged, but of which neither names nor details affected the poet. Besides, what did the monarchist and Catholic cause matter to him then? It was to take thirteen years of a new and formidable war to make him desire the restoration of the Bourbons. Annette's arguments and explanations jarred with his own opinions. Much as he might admire the bravery of the loyal monarchist, and be moved

---

[1] Sonnet: " Once did she hold . . ."
[2] Sonnet: " Toussaint, the most unhappy . . ."
[3] Sonnet: " We had a female passenger . . ."

by her perils and misfortunes, he could not but
blame morals and habits which were suggested by
Annette's narratives, whatever might be her reserve
in the telling.

How far away he felt her to be from what now
made up his whole life, not only from nature, but
from poetry as he understood and practised it!
Between them stood the barrier of language; never
could she delight in the verses he had written, nor
in those he still would write; never would she grasp
their rhythm nor their beauty; even if he translated
them to her, scarcely could she catch at a few of
the ideas that had inspired him, and those ideas,
strange and subtle as they were, were more likely to
bewilder than to enchant her. His daughter herself
did not know English, and he despaired of ever
making her intellectually and poetically his child.
Besides, in the long interval which had elapsed since
1792 he had lost the fluency and readiness of his
French. To speak it was now a painful effort, words
and accentuation played him false.

To balance these impressions of profound disappointment he would have had to feel some renewal
of the old fascination, a rekindling of the ashes of
his sensuous and exalted passion. Alas! Annette
was now thirty-six, and aged, no doubt, by anxieties
and trials. He, on the other hand, was still a young
man, and shielded from her influence by a new love;
all he could feel for her was a remnant of affection
compounded of gratitude for the past, of pity for
the present.

With the wisdom and calm which the years
had brought, they were, moreover, probably both
agreed on rejecting the idea of a permanent union.

Circumstances, against which they had railed so long, had on the whole been merciful in holding them apart. The ten years they had lived away from each other had opened an impassable gulf between their tastes and habits, or rather had brought to light the essential difference of their natures. Annette, no less than William, now realised the impossibility of a life in common. She would have been deeply grieved at parting from her friends at Blois, to whom she was bound by the ties of common hopes, fears and perils. She would have been terrified at the idea of the hostile island, where a language unknown to her was spoken, where (to judge by William and Dorothy, in spite of all their friendly attentions) the people had their own ways of seeing and feeling, their own emotions and pleasures which were so different from hers.

Both showed rare wisdom in confirming their separation, and still greater wisdom in parting in friendship with kind thoughts towards each other. Indeed this equanimity was possible only because passion was dead. There subsisted only the memory of the past which seems to have remained with them untroubled by poignant regrets. The whole story ended without any ill-feeling, with a certain sweetness veiled by a shadow of sadness. We read in Dorothy's diary on 29th August, the very day of the Wordsworths' return to Dover: " We sate upon the Dover cliffs, and looked upon France with many a melancholy and tender thought."

What had been agreed upon between Wordsworth and Annette? Wo do not know. Neither do we know what steps he took to assist the mother of his child, nor the offers he had made. It may be that

Wordsworth, fearing for Caroline the influence of Annette's combativity, proposed to take charge of his daughter after having come to an agreement with Mary Hutchinson, who was capable in her generous kindness of being a mother to her.   But neither Annette nor Caroline, who were all in all to one another, could consent to this change.   The help proffered by Wordsworth for his child's education then took another form, of which we have no evidence.   Was it immediate and effectual?   Or was it the promise of a yearly help soon cancelled by circumstances?   It was not till the following year that the Earl of Lonsdale was to repay the money owed by his father.   Wordsworth had received nothing of it when he saw Annette at Calais.   If he was content with a mere promise, what was the outcome of it later on?   Eight months after their meeting, war broke out anew, and all communication between them was once more cut off.

The one thing certain is that Caroline remained with her of whom circumstances had made her doubly the daughter.   She remained French and spoke the language of France.

The Calais interview was the decisive crisis of the love of Wordsworth and Annette.   They were to remain friends to the end—friends, but never husband and wife.   William was to marry Mary, and eventually did so on 4th October.   Annette was to go back to Blois with Caroline.   The former lovers saw one another only once again, eighteen years afterwards.

XIV

ANNETTE now returned to her friends, the Chouans of Blois, who in spite of their ever-dwindling hopes, kept up their hostile manœuvres against the Chief Consul. But most of her troubles were caused for a time by her brother Paul. Though they now weighed more heavily on her, their origin dated far back, and she may have told part of them to Wordsworth during her interview with him.

When the capital sentence pronounced on Paul in 1793 had been cancelled, he had gone back to Orleans again to fill his post of notary's clerk in Maître Courtois's office. But he did not recover his balance for a time. He was then in the state of mind of many who gave themselves up wholly and passionately to pleasure as a compensation for their past anxieties. To his misfortune he made in 1795 the acquaintance of a certain " Mme. de Bonneuil," whose beauty and whose alleged brilliant connections were then setting the hearts of the youth of Orleans on fire.[1] She was, as a matter of fact, a woman of the name of Rifflon whose father was a skinner at Bourges. She had had countless love intrigues, several of them with members of the nobility and famous people whose names gave prestige to her tales. Among many others she quoted the names of M. de Bellegarde, described as an extravagant spendthrift as far as women were concerned, whom she knew at Versailles under the old regime; more

[1] The whole Bonneuil episode is related from papers in the *Archives nationales*, F⁷ 6340. The main facts are gathered from Paul Vallon's declarations to the police.

recently, in Madrid, she had been connected with the French ambassador, M. de Pérignon; M. de Villequier, the agent of the Bourbons, and Godoy, the prince of the Peace, of whom she had simultaneously been the mistress. She complacently showed letters from Godoy; she also exhibited some from the late Prince Louis of Prussia.

She was pretty, and was mistress of the art of preserving her beauty, to the point of unblushingly giving herself out as twenty years younger than she was. Gifted with a genius for intrigue, she gave such excellent reasons for her movement, she excelled to such an extent in confusing people's minds that the wonderful Consulate police itself seems not to have seen very clearly what her game was.

Paul made her acquaintance at the house of a certain Maugus, a lodging-house keeper, who lived in the Place du Martroi, and had formed a literary society called " Cracovie," where the newspapers were read. He lived with her until she forsook him for other conquests. But that period of dissipation made regular work wearisome and the life at Orleans distasteful to him. Either because Maître Courtois no longer appreciated his services, or because the metropolis attracted him, he left Orleans for Paris in 1800. There he occupied several posts, never stopping long in any, staying for instance three months with M. de Lasteyrie, the famous agriculturist, who was then writing on Spanish sheep. Finally he took work with Maître Thierry, a notary at Melun, and was there when, during a short journey he took to Paris, he found himself again in the presence of Madame de Bonneuil. The old passion flamed up again on the spot. She was going, she told him, to Spain with 40,000 francs' worth of goods, lace and false pearls. She offered to take him as her assistant or secretary. He consented. At least such is the explanation of the adventure that Paul gave to the police, but it is likely that under the cover of these business trans-actions, a Bourbon intrigue was hidden.

Their passports, which have been preserved with their descriptions, are interesting. Madame de Bon-neuil declares herself to be twenty-nine, but a marginal note from the police makes the correction: " She is nearly fifty." One may, however, imagine her a pretty woman with brown hair, well-made nose, small mouth, round chin, round face and high colour. As for Paul Vallon, he wears a brown wig; he is but five feet four inches; he has grey eyes under a high forehead barred by dark eyebrows.

They went first to Spain, where they stayed from March to August 1802, that is until the month that Wordsworth and Annette spent together in Calais. From the very start, they had strange ups and downs. She sold lace. She again tried the batteries of her charms on the prince of the Peace in order to obtain from him permission to export piastres, but fortune soon wearied of her. She went on to Portugal. There they passed through a time of hardships, and Paul, according to a family tradition, in order to earn his living had to load orange ships in the port of Lisbon. From Portugal they went to England, whence, after spending three months in London, they sailed for Holland. They spent all the winter together—from November 1802 to March 1803—either in Amster-dam or at The Hague. But at that date, the Consulate police began to feel uneasy on the subject of the adventuress and to suspect her of political intrigues.

Her passage through London had made her an object of suspicion. No doubt peace with England was not yet broken, but everyone knew it was but a truce between two deadly enemies. As early as 21st January, 1803, the High Commissioner for the commercial relations of the French Republic in Holland addressed from Amsterdam a report to Semonville, the French ambassador at The Hague, warning the latter of Madame de Bonneuil's arrival in Amsterdam on 18th November with " a person sixteen or seventeen years old, of charming appearance, whom she calls her niece and treats pretty badly; an Englishman about forty, tolerably well looking, of average size, who styles himself Lord Spenser, and finally a little, dark, rather ill-looking man, about thirty years old, who is called Vallon, and whom she passes off as her secretary. . . ." She keeps up a very active correspondence: " Besides a secretary who does not leave her and seems very busy, she herself writes ceaselessly."

Paul Vallon must have left her in March 1803 to go back to Paris. We do not know if he was still with her on 13th March when Madame de Bonneuil was first visited by detective Mackenem. This agent, who seems to have had a turn for humour, has left us curious and detailed accounts of his conversations with the adventuress.

She was suspected by the Chief Consul of plotting with the English against his life. Mackenem introduced himself to her as a *ci-devant* (former nobleman) ruined by the Revolution, but formerly very intimate with Bonaparte, who had not withdrawn his confidence from him. Madame de Bonneuil, on her side, claimed to have a secret plot to divulge to

PAUL VALLON

the Chief Consul, but to him only, which concerned
some Englishmen who intended to murder him. The
detective expressed surprise that " they should have
chosen a pretty woman like her as confidante of such
horrors." "Here, assuming a modest countenance, she
confessed to me, with pain (she said), that it was to
her poor charms that she owed her knowledge of this
infamous secret." Her beauty had excited rivalry
between two men who were taking the lead in this
matter, and had betrayed each other out of hatred.
The English, then, had put a price of three thousand
guineas and a pension upon Bonaparte's head. As
Mackenem seemed doubtful, she offered to let him
see her next-door neighbour, Colonel Spenser, one
of the conspirators. And in fact, the said Colonel
appeared as if by magic. There followed a conversation in English between him and the lady, of which
Mackenem did not understand a single word—no
more than Spenser understood her when she spoke
French with Mackenem. She repeated to each
whatever she chose. Throughout she tried to pass
herself off on Mackenem as a patriot working for the
good of Bonaparte.

Mackenem continued to follow up her traces. He
tried to catch her up at Pyrmont in the Principality
of Waldeck, and sent a very amusing report from
Hanover to General Moncey, inspector-general of
the police, on 13th August.

Before reaching Pyrmont, he had learned that
Madame de Bonneuil had just taken public leave of
the society of that watering-place at a ball given by
the Prince of Brunswick. She had particularly insisted on saying good-bye to the Bavarian Electress
" before going," so she said, " to Gotha." There was

not a moment to lose.   Mackenem showed his credentials to the Prince of Waldeck and asked him to expel from his court the adventuress who, " as vile as her birth, is impudent enough to introduce herself into society where she can maintain herself only by dint of lying and fraud."

" Ah! " the prince said to me, " in a public place such as Pyrmont, when you see a woman, you do not ask who she is nor where she comes from, but only whether she is young and pretty."   " As to being pretty," I replied, " it may be she is thought so, but as regards youth, I have known her for at least twenty years as a very active courtesan, and very dangerous intriguer."   " Ah! " said His Highness to me, " she is at most thirty-five."   " Admitting this to be the case," I said, " Your Highness, being a soldier, must know that for a soldier the campaigning years are reckoned double."   The prince laughed and said: " Since you insist on going to Pyrmont, I will give instructions. . . ."

And indeed Mackenem gained his point and was taken in a post-chaise to Pyrmont, but he was driven along circuitous and abominable roads, while an express hurried straight away by a direct route to warn Madame de Bonneuil.   When the exhausted detective arrived, she had fled into Prussian territory.   Poor Mackenem, in order to uphold the prestige of the consular police, had to invent an errand in search of lodgings at Pyrmont for his sick wife, which left him no choice but to take up his quarters in the small watering-place from which the clever bird had flown.

XV

PAUL VALLON, as we saw, was no longer with the adventuress. He had left her before the renewal of hostilities in May 1803. He was in Paris, leading a dissipated and precarious existence. He had no money, and was looking about for a situation with the help of M. Bonvalet, a business agent in the Place Vendôme, who was making inquiries about him at Blois and trying to get a post for him.

However, closely watched by the police, he was arrested on 2nd July, and that very day underwent a preliminary cross-examination; he underwent another on the 16th. The authorities wanted to get out of him information about Madame de Bonneuil. But he claimed to know nothing of her political intrigues. He merely kept her books and commercial correspondence. " He did not notice she had suspicious liaisons with foreigners, with English people." Since his return to Paris he had heard nothing whatever from her.

It must be concluded that notwithstanding his monarchist relations, the personal innocence of Paul appeared manifest to the police, for on 5th October he was released from Ste. Pélagie where he had been imprisoned. He was free, but his connection with Madame de Bonneuil leaving some apprehension behind, he was ordered out of Paris and forced to live at Blois under the prefect's supervision. But how was he to live? He could not return to Paris where he had friends and might find a situation. Nor could he indefinitely live at the expense of his family in Blois. Paul was hopeless. His fate seemed almost desperate, when the strategic genius of one of his sisters—probably Annette—helped him out.[1] In January 1804 Paul came, accompanied by her, to the market-town of St. Dyé, on the Loire, a little above Blois, to take possession of a small legacy. In this very town lived the notary Puzéla, a well-known monarchist, whose adventures under the Revolution have been related by his daughter, Marie Catherine, in her *Memoirs*, lately published.

Louis Puzéla (1748–1806), a passionate devotee of the royalist and Catholic cause, had plunged with gloomy zeal into the fight against the Revolution. He had undergone more than four months' imprisonment under the Terror, and his elder daughter, Marie Catherine, then seventeen years old, in order to alleviate the physical sufferings of a sickly father, and to support him with her filial love, had of her own free will shared his imprisonment. Unexpectedly set free, Puzéla had settled as a notary at St. Dyé, where he lived with his heroic daughter and her younger sister, upon both of whom his ascetic and sullen temper imposed a trying restraint. Unable to bear the thought of seeing them exposed to ungodly temptations, he forbade all kinds of amusement. He would not hear of the elder girl trying to divert her thoughts by music or reading. The mere idea that she might marry was odious to him. He employed her as his clerk so that no young man should have access to his house. Moreover, his fanaticism made everyone avoid him. In his eyes hardly any of the St. Dyé families were zealous

[1] The following pages are grounded on *Mémoires de Madame Vallon*, edited by Guy Trouillard, 1913, chiefly from pp 222–9.

enough for the " good cause." Raboteau, an agent of the Directory, wrote on 17th November, 1797 :[1]

If he had had his way, our unhappy country would have become another Vendée. The non-juring priests and even the deported ones, of whom he was the zealous friend, found at his house lodging, a chapel and supporters of their fatal errors. . . . He has two young ladies worthy from their manners to be " *ci-devant* duchesses," who, just like their dear father, only visit the most respectable houses."

Raboteau had certainly no idea of what the " duchesses " suffered under the enforced regime. Marie Catherine was falling into a decline. She finally fell ill, and came dangerously near to death. A famous Parisian physician, Dr. Chambon de Montaux, was then at Blois, but he had, in the capacity of Mayor of Paris in 1793, been a member of the commission that had to notify to the king the death sentence passed by the Convention. It mattered not that he should have resigned his functions immediately afterwards, and that he had been persecuted by the Terrorists. To Puzéla, he was no better than a regicide. " For his own sake," his daughter tells us, " he would rather have died than see him, but for mine he consented." Here we must quote a page from the *Memoirs* :

M. Chambon came. He stayed by me a whole day, watched my illness, told my father that so far as he could judge it was due to a kind of life little fitted to one of my sex, age and disposition; and that he must prepare himself to lose me in a very short time if he made me work on in the same way. My father was crushed. This

[1] *Mémoires de Madame Vallon*, p. 216.

G

sentence ruined all his plans, but he loved me too much
to sacrifice me.

During my convalescence, which was very long, your
father [that is Paul Vallon : she is writing for her children]
came out of the prison of Ste. Pélagie where he had been
detained since his return from foreign countries. A small
legacy necessitated his presence at St. Dyé. His parents
were living at Blois and one of his sisters accompanied
him. The fame of my father was great. The political
opinions of the sister were said to be very good, and
although she did not know us, she introduced her brother;
the victims of the Revolution told their misfortunes to
each other and were soon fast friends. Your father confided to mine that he was watched by the police and that
he could stay nowhere unless with special permission.
To attempt disobedience was to defy the tyrants.

His sister had heard of the presumed cause of my
illness. Her brother had been for fifteen years a head
clerk at Orleans and was a very talented man. She proposed our marriage to my father. Still dazed by the blow
delivered to him by M. Chambon, circumvented by the
sister, who gave him no time to breathe and continually
represented the monarchist alliance as worthy of him, my
father, who had sworn in his heart never to let me marry,
was persuaded. To his mind, there was no need of his
daughter's consent: they settled everything, and then your
father was introduced to me as my destined husband.
I was morally very weak at that time and physically
weaker still, for I remember I could not rise from a large
easy chair to welcome brother and sister. I agreed to
everything with a feeling of joy.

Three weeks later I married your father. . . .

The thing is perhaps a little less strange than
Mademoiselle Puzéla thought it. Her father's name
in 1797–1800 had been on the same list of suspected
Chouans as Annette, " the widow William." Both

were well known to Guyon de Montlivault, who was a visitor at the house of the Vallon sisters, and at the same time was the protector of Puzéla; it was Montlivault who had forced the unwilling inhabitants, or rather the republicans, to accept him as notary at St. Dyé. He may have answered for the opinions of the Vallons to Puzéla.

Moreover, Dr. Chambon, who in 1798 was candidate for the post of civil doctor at the Blois Hospital, surely knew the medical man who was head of that hospital—Charles Henry Vallon. He may have spoken to him of the sick girl at St. Dyé and of the urgency of finding a husband for her. It may be Annette had heard of these circumstances before leaving Blois.

That she is the sister of Paul spoken of in the *Memoirs* in this connection is extremely likely, although there can be no certainty about it; her close intimacy with Paul, her royalist activities, more pronounced than those of her sisters—everything points to her. And, indeed, she displayed in the matter a genius which recalls that of her enemy Bonaparte. Like him she knew how to prepare an offensive movement with wonderful rapidity and win a victory, crushing in its immediate effect, but making ultimately for the benefit of both parties. Thanks to her, Marie Catherine Puzéla was to be rescued from the illness which was thought fatal. As to Paul, who was drifting, though we may consider that, after his lapses, he obtained in the pious heroine a gift above his deserts, though we may suspect that his rash adventure with Madame de Bonneuil was in the telling somewhat transfigured into an episode of pure *chouannerie*, into a bold attempt to overthrow the Chief Consul, he was yet to make himself worthy of

his mate by his transformed life. The secretary of
the equivocal Madame de Bonneuil was to become an
accomplished notary, a perfect husband, the father of
four children destined to enter honourable careers:
three sons, one a prefect, another a barrister, the
third a judge; a daughter who married first a notary,
then a *Conseiller à la Cour*.

His good behaviour is certified by the very man
who was set to supervise him, Prefect Corbigny.[1]
This prefect was clever, temperate, courteous and
slightly sceptical. A Breton by birth, being given
at twenty-two a mission in Brittany during the
Terror, he managed to prevent excesses in his
district. Appointed Prefect of Loir-et-Cher at the
age of twenty-nine, he was able in a short time to
calm down excited spirits and to reconcile contending
parties. He rallied to the new regime many stubborn
opponents by his efforts to restore to all the emigrants
of his department such of their estates as had not
been sold. He was averse from all violence. He was
no fanatic in politics, and he carried out his functions
with a regretful eye on the literary studies of his
youth. Was he not the author of two tragedies, a
few comedies and some poems? When he died in
1811, a baron of the Empire, peace reigned in the
department formerly so turbulent.

Paul Vallon found in him no churlish jailer. When
he had reported to him on arriving at Blois, Corbigny
no doubt looked with some curiosity at the friend of

---

[1] On Corbigny see *Biographie Universelle et Portative des
Contemporains ou Dictionnaire historique des hommes vivants
et des hommes morts depuis 1788 jusqu'à nos jours, publié sous
la direction de MM. Rabbe, Vieilh de Boisjolin et Ste. Preuve*
four vols., Paris, 1834.

Madame de Bonneuil committed to his guard. At first sight he judged that his wild oats were sown. As early as 10th December, 1803, he wrote to the Secretary of State for Justice, who had ordered him to undertake an inquiry:

The information I have gathered about Paul Vallon shows him to be a respectable man whose head has been turned by certain events of the Revolution, but who is now sobered down. There is no doubt that his behaviour at Blois, since I had the opportunity of watching him, gives no ground for uneasiness. I have nothing but favourable reports to make of him since that time.

Yet there were a few weeks at the beginning of his married life, when Paul all but took another rash step. He could not bear at first the idea of settling near his austere father-in-law. In spite of the efforts of his wife to palliate the matter in her *Memoirs*, we catch a hint of early differences of opinion.

Your father [she writes to her children] lived on fairly good terms with mine; the conformity of their opinions made up for the difference of tastes, but your father loved society, whereas mine only enjoyed his home. . . . He [M. Puzéla] had given up all his rights over his daughters, but he did not realise it.

Thus Paul, only recently married, asked (25th February, 1804) to be released from supervision and from internment in the department of Loir-et-Cher. He needed, he said, to reside in Paris for business reasons. He had a partner in Paris. He could not find means of livelihood at Blois. It seems that while applying for release, he did not wait for the application to be granted, for the prefect thought it necessary to threaten him with arrest. This caused great terror to his young wife, from whom they had till then hidden the fact that he was under police supervision. She writes:

There were folk charitable enough to tell me that the Prefect of Loir-et-Cher meant to have your father arrested because he dared to leave St. Dyé. I was thunderstruck at the prospect of seeing the prisons again open their doors. In a great state of terror I spoke of it to my father, who then told me everything and added: " Your husband has thirteen years of persecution to his credit, my daughter: I needed these qualifications in my son-in-law."

I went to call on the prefect, to whom I must do justice. He said to me: " I wanted to give your husband a lesson of prudence by threatening him. In compelling him to continue to live near you, I am not hard on him. Be comforted, madam, I entrust your husband to you. Go and consult the police registers, and you will see what testimonials I have given in favour of his establishment." So I did; his report was most flattering to me, and most moderate in respect of the political conduct of my father and husband.

The adroitness and moderation of the courteous prefect succeeded splendidly. Paul resigned himself; entered into partnership with his father-in-law, and succeeded him as notary when Puzéla died two years later.

Yet the police remained suspicious. In spite of a new and favourable report from the prefect on 30th October, 1804, in which it is stated that Paul Vallon " has behaved properly since coming to Blois, that he has married, and is working with his father-in-law, a notary, which inclines us to think that he means to lead a quiet life," the Secretary of State postponed the examination of Paul's request to be liberated.

As long as the Empire endured Paul remained, curiously enough, at once a notary and a suspected man under police supervision. He obtained his entire freedom only at the Restoration.

XVI

THE consequence of his being placed under supervision was to turn once more the attention of the police towards his sisters, one of whom had an English name. After the " infernal machine," and the discovery of Cadoudal's plot, the secret police, on the look-out for all the Chief Consul's enemies, pointed out, on 8th March, 1804, to the Loir-et-Cher prefect as requiring " particular supervision, the following citizens: *Lacaille*, a gunsmith, and his two sons, *Rancogne* the younger—*alias* Charles—formerly captain under Georges (Cadoudal), *Pardessus*, the younger, son of a barrister, *Montlivau* (*sic*), a returned emigrant," finally " the *demoiselles Vallon*, one of whom is married to an Englishman named Willaume (*sic*). We are told that the aforesaid individuals often meet in her house. I direct you, as prefect, to have their conduct carefully observed, and to let me know the results of the observation and your own opinion regarding them." [1]

Corbigny answered on 16th March, to the " Councillor of State specially in charge of examining and following up all the affairs connected with the

---

[1] Archives nationales, F⁷ 6410, 5ᵉ division: Police secrète, Dossier n° 8171.

tranquillity and internal security of the Republic."
Regarding the Vallon sisters, he says:

The *Vallon* sisters, as well as their sister Madame
Williams (*sic*) have always been known as friends and
abettors of the royalists. They have a brother who is
under supervision in my department and who was
for a long time imprisoned in the Temple prison on
account of journeys he had made into foreign parts with
Madame de Bonneuil. The woman Williams particularly
is known as an active intriguer. The police commissary
of Blois assures me there are no suspicious meetings in
that house. As I have only to-day returned to my
department I cannot give more positive information
in the matter, but I am going to arrange for a watch to
be set on them which will let me know all that is done
at their house.[1]

The prefect ends by reducing the affair to modest
proportions. He admits that there is in the department a fairly large number of supporters of the
Bourbons who would try to turn to their advantage
" an event such as the one we were threatened by,
that is the Chief Consul's death," but at bottom there
is nothing to be anxious about:

Their well-known weakness of character, the strength
of the government, the firmness of the administration,
and the comfort they enjoy, will prevent them, I think,
from making any criminal attempt, but it is essential to
watch their doings closely as their political opinions,
generally speaking, are unsatisfactory. You may depend
on me that no pains will be spared to prove to them that
there is nothing to be gained by nursing foolish hopes.

The prefect also admits in that very letter of

[1] Archives nationales, F⁷ 6410, 5ᵉ division: Police secrète,
Dossier n° 8171.

16th November, 1804, in which he notes the good behaviour of Paul, that " the family of the Sieur Vallon and that of his wife have been known since the beginning of the Revolution, for political opinions and habits of intrigue which have always been in favour of the old order."

Yet his own policy was not to punish, but to disarm and conciliate. He succeeded in his aim. Two of the uncompromising supporters of the Bourbons who were suspected of frequenting the house of the *demoiselles* Vallon were soon to make their peace with the new regime. Guyon de Montlivault became chief secretary of Madame Bonaparte (for which error he made amends in 1815, when he was conspicuous among the most fervid *ultras*). As to Jean Marie Pardessus, he became deputy-mayor of Blois in 1804, and mayor in 1805. We find him a deputy to the Legislative Assembly in 1807, and in 1810 the Imperial Government appointed him Professor of Commercial Law in Paris, the first stage of his career as a famous jurisconsult. No doubt he remained a monarchist at heart, but he dropped all active hostility against the Empire.

Annette and her sisters, who remained firm in their faith, must have suffered from these desertions. Powerless and isolated, they were leading a quiet life. The turbulent Annette herself, who, on account of her English name, felt the weight of a double suspicion, kept quiet and devoted herself to the education of her daughter. We know nothing more of her until the fall of the Empire. War had barred all possible communications between herself and Wordsworth.

Only a few domestic events in the house in the Rue du Pont are known to us: the death within a few months in 1805 of her stepfather, Dr. Vergez, and of her mother, and four years later the death of the second of the three sisters, Adélaïde Angélique. Were those losses the reason for which Annette left the family house, or did she do so on account of the abdication of Napoleon in 1814? Whatever the reason, it is in Paris that we find Annette and Caroline settled at the Restoration.

XVII

WHEN Napoleon resigned his throne at Fontaine-bleau, on 14th April, 1814, it was news as joyful to Wordsworth as to Annette. Both had fought in their own way—the one by prose and verse, the other by intrigue—against " the usurper." The conclusion of the long war also enabled them to resume a correspondence of which war had been the sole interrupter. The poet could not think of France without calling up the image of his former mistress and their child. He remained anxious for their safety, although his affections had long since ceased to be concentrated on them. His English family, with their joys and sorrows, were becoming all in all to him. The sweet tenderness of Mary was sinking deeper and deeper into his heart. Indeed he had chosen wisely. True, she had none of the brilliant qualities which the world admires and which fascinate people at first sight. But now that he saw the " very pulsations of her being," he knew all her worth. She was endowed with the true beauty, that of the soul, which only discloses itself to loving eyes:

Heed not tho' none should call thee fair;
   So, Mary, let it be
If nought in loveliness compare
   With what thou art to me.

True beauty dwells in deep retreats,
   Whose veil is unremoved
Till heart with heart in concord beats,
   And the lover is beloved.[1]

The quietude of Mary[2] effaced the memory of
Annette. The five children she bore the poet during
the Empire—those children who grew up under his
eyes, whose caresses he loved, through whom too he
learned to know deep sorrow, for he saw two of them
die in 1812—made the image of the eldest daughter,
the ever absent Caroline, recede into a hazy distance.

Indifference? Observation of propriety? Or mere
laziness? He relaxed the only bond still linking him
to his French daughter and to her mother. He no
longer wrote to them personally. When the correspondence was resumed, his sister Dorothy did so in
his place. It was she who, with the little French she
knew, answered Annette's letters. If Wordsworth
correctly performed, when circumstances demanded
it, his paternal duty, Dorothy felt and showed a real
kinship with Caroline, " her niece," as she tenderly
calls her.

Neither her letters nor Annette's have come down

---

[1] " Let other bards of angels sing."

[2] " Her words were few. In reality, she talked so little that
Mr. Slave-Trade Clarkson used to allege against her that she
could only say ' God bless you! ' . . . How much better this
was adapted to her husband's taste, than a blue-stocking
loquacity, or even a legitimate talent for discussion."—De
Quincey's *Lake Poets.* Ed. David Masson, 1889, Vol. II. p. 236.

to us, but we hear an echo of them in Dorothy's correspondence with her friend Mrs. Clarkson, the wife of the anti-slavery apostle, which has been published by Professor Harper.

We learn from it that a young officer named Eustace Baudouin visited the Wordsworths at Rydal Mount, and that Baudouin was a prisoner of war liberated by the recent peace.[1]   The brother of a colonel of the Imperial Army, he had been sent to the military school of St. Cyr and thence to Spain as a sub-lieutenant at the age of nineteen. He had scarcely had time to show his valour there when he was thrice wounded, was taken prisoner at Olot in Catalonia, on 13th April, 1811, and soon after sent to England.   There, during three years of captivity, he had at the same time an opportunity of learning the language and of making the acquaintance of the Wordsworths.   His relations with them became close enough for Dorothy to call him in 1814, " our friend Baudouin." [2] It is probable that when peace re-opened to him the gates of France, he was entrusted by the poet with some message for Annette. Thence sprang up between the Vallon and Baudouin families a rapid intimacy. Besides the colonel, Eustace had another brother, Jean Baptiste Martin, then head of an office at the Mont de Piété. The latter, who was thirty-three years old, fell in love with Caroline Wordsworth, who was twenty-one, asked her in marriage and was accepted. It is this marriage which is the

---

[1] Ministère de la Guerre: Archives administratives.

[2] It was without doubt his frequent presence at Rydal Mount that later on gave the Coleridges the impression that Wordsworth had had a *son*, not a daughter, in France. Eustace Baudouin was exactly of the same age as Caroline.

chief argument of Dorothy's first letters to Mrs. Clarkson after the Restoration:

She [Caroline] and her mother [Dorothy writes on 9th October, 1814] are extremely anxious that I should be present at the wedding and for that purpose have pressed me very much to go in October. This, unless such good fortune attended us as being taken under your and your Husband's protection, we could not think of at this season, and therefore I wish that the marriage should be deferred till next spring or summer, because I desire exceedingly to see the poor Girl before she takes another protector than her mother, under whom I believe she has been bred up in perfect purity and innocence, and to whom she is light and life and perpetual pleasure; though, from the over-generous dispositions of the mother, they have had to struggle through many difficulties. Well, I began to say that I particularly wished that you could have seen them at this time, as through you I should have been able to enter into some explanations, which, imperfectly as I express myself in French, are difficult, and as you would have been able to confirm or contradict the reports that we receive from Caroline's Mother and Mr. Beaudouin (sic) of her interesting and amiable qualities. They both say that she resembles her Father most strikingly, and her letters give a picture of a feeling and ingenuous mind. Yet there must be something, I think, very unfavourable to true delicacy in French manners. Both Caroline and her Mother urge my going in October on this account, that, after a young woman is once engaged to be married, it is desirable that the delay afterwards should be as short as possible, as she is subject to perpetual scrutiny and unpleasant remarks, and one of the reasons they urge for marriage in general is that a single woman in France, unless she have a fortune, is not treated with any *consideration*.[1]

[1] Harper's *William Wordsworth*, II. pp. 211-12.

Dorothy is anxious about the journey. Though the Clarksons assure her they found a kind welcome in Paris from the French people, she cannot help thinking that " their judgment is formed on the best of the people," for accounts from all other quarters depict the French as " rude and brutal in their manners." She would fain have M. Baudouin meet her at Calais, but is frightened at the expense this plan would involve:

We should wish to carry presents of English manufacture. Can this be done without much risk or disagreeable trouble?

On 31st December she announces her journey for April 1815, but as she expects to stay in France at least nine or ten weeks, she is afraid of the disturbances which are sure to occur during the king's coronation:

Besides the journey will be very expensive, which we can ill afford, and the money would be better spent in augmenting my Niece's wedding portion. To this effect I have written to her. She would not consent to marry without my presence, which was the reason that April was fixed

If she were not troubled at the thought of leaving her brother and her sister-in-law, she would think of the journey " with satisfaction—nay, with delight, for that dear young woman's sake whom I believe to be thoroughly amiable." [1]

But Napoleon returns from Elba, and the plans for the marriage and journey are all upset. As early as 16th March, before the Emperor reached Paris, and

[1] Harper's *William Wordsworth*, II. pp. 213-14.

while the success of his attempt was still doubtful, Dorothy had written to Mrs. Clarkson:

For the sake of our Friends I am truly distressed. The lady whom I mentioned to you from the first was a zealous Royalist, has often risked her life in defence of adherents to that cause, and she despised and detested Buonaparte. Poor creature! In the last letter we had from her she spoke only of hope and comfort; said that the king's government was daily gaining strength, and Buonaparte's friends [coming over] in their hearts to the other side. A few days after the [evil tidings] reached her she would receive my letter containing the plan of our journey.[1]

Less than one month later, on 11th April, Napoleon having again become the master of France, Dorothy again writes saying she cannot sleep for thinking about the evils that the Emperor's " fiendish ambition " will set loose:

Everybody here is anxious, but none a hundredth part so much as we are. We had a long letter from France written on the 19th and 20th. The letter was concluded at midnight. My Friend says: " I hear troops entering the City. I think it is the *avant-garde* of Buonaparte. Good God! What is to become of us? " We have had another letter written the next day in miserable dejection; but she says no more of public affairs than that " all is quiet." Lodgings were taken for us in the " Hôtel du Jardin Turc, Boulevard du Temple, in a pleasant part of Paris," as they describe it. Poor creatures, they say they are shipwrecked when just entering into port. Indeed it is a distressful situation, but I trust that we shall see them in Paris before the end of another twelvemonth.

[1] Harper's *William Wordsworth*, II. pp. 214-15.
[2] Harper's *William Wordsworth*, II. p. 215.

Annette was again the fearless Chouanne of old in the fight against Napoleon. The Baron de Tardif, testifying in 1816 to Annette's indomitable royalism, describes her conduct during the Hundred Days in these terms:

During the last events which plunged France into mourning, she performed acts of courage, with no interested motives. Conscious only of her attachment to the legitimate dynasty, she posted proclamations at night, distributed them in the day-time, favoured the escape of the brave men who wanted to devote themselves to the king's service.[1]

Her merit was the greater, in that many of her political friends bowed to the new imperial order. Guyon de Montlivault paid his court to Napoleon after his return. Nicolas Bailly signed the Address from the Cour de Cassation to the returning Emperor in spite of just having signified his adherence to his deposition. The jurisconsult Pardessus himself wrote an address to Napoleon, an act which he recanted a few months afterwards in Parliament:

" I was very guilty, but I asked pardon of my king, and my king forgave me." " On your knees then," said M. de Girardin laughing. " With a wax-candle in your hand," cried M. de Kératry.[2]

It is pleasing to see that Annette was guilty of no such weakness. She was guided, not by interest, but by her monarchist faith.

[1] See Appendix: The Baron de Tardif, who gives that praise to Annette, certifies the same of Eustace Baudouin, who (says de Tardif) " was entrusted with the exhibition of all posters destined to bring back the people to their king " (*Archives du Ministère de la Guerre*).

[2] *Biographie Universelle et Portative*, etc., op. cit.

At the same time, the Waterloo campaign roused the anxieties of the Wordsworths. Their hatred of Napoleon, and alas! of France, reached its climax. The new victory of the Allies did not soothe their violent anger. The good Dorothy, echoing the poet who was about to write that *Thanksgiving Ode* of his, which might have been inspired by the Holy Alliance itself, makes an attack in her letter of 15th August on the English admirers of France, and adds: "Would that all the English had Prussian hearts, and that our generals and counsellors had the soul of Blücher!"[1] She then goes on to give news of Annette:

It is impossible for me to think of going to Paris this year. We have had letters from our Friends written just after the return of the king. They were in great joy at that event, and urged me and my companions to go, all being safe and quiet. At the same time they waited our determination respecting Caroline's coming over. We could only answer that the time of meeting my Br. and Sr. was gone by, and that we could not appoint any particular plan, knowing of nobody about to return from Paris, and having no friends in London to whom we could with propriety entrust her, but we proposed that the Mother should look out for some person or persons coming to London, to whose care she might be consigned till we could hear from her of her arrival there. This I trust may not be difficult, as Madame Vallon has a numerous acquaintance. I wish you had been in London in lodgings. The great difficulty will be there; for people who might be relied upon for the journey must be continually coming from Paris.[2]

[1] Harper's *William Wordsworth*, II. p. 216.
[2] Harper's *William Wordsworth*, II. pp. 216–17.

H

XVIII

OWING to continual postponements on the part of the Wordsworths, the wedding finally took place without Caroline having been to see her father in England, and without any of the Wordsworths being present at the ceremony.

The wedding was celebrated on 28th February, 1816, at noon, at the *Mairie* of the 3rd *arrondissement*. Annette wanted the ceremony to be impressive and summoned her brilliant friends from far and near. They willingly answered the summons, wishing to acknowledge the services rendered to the Bourbon cause by the valiant Chouanne of Blois. The wedding had all the appearance of a royalist manifestation.

In the marriage certificate, the spelling of the bride's name was duly corrected and the former error pointed out. It is true other mistakes were made in its stead. Caroline was spoken of as the " *fille majeure* (of age) of Williams (*sic*) Wordsworth, *propriétaire*, living at Grasner Kendan (*sic*), duchy of Westermorland (*sic*)."

Among the witnesses were the bridegroom's brother, Eustace Baudouin of St. Étienne, head instructor of the Scotch company, *Chevalier de la Légion d'honneur*, and former prosecutor of Babeuf; and Nicolas Bailly, chevalier, *Officier de la Légion d'honneur*, councillor of the Cour de Cassation.

The wedding was consecrated at St. Vincent de Paul, the church on the hill, whose broad successive flights of stairs lend themselves so admirably to the ascent of a brilliant procession.

In spite of her very limited resources, Annette had insisted on giving a great dinner, to which she had invited the largest number she possibly could

of the notable people she knew. On this occasion
she wrote a letter to the Wordsworths, in which she
took pleasure in describing to them all the pomp
that had attended the marriage of the poet's daughter.
Dorothy communicated the substance of the letter
to Mrs. Clarkson on 4th April:

The mother's details of the wedding festivities would
have amused you. She was to give the fête, she who
perhaps for half a year to come will feel the effects of it
at every dinner she cooks! Thirty persons were present
to dinner, ball and supper. The deputies of the department and many other respectable people were there.
The bride was dressed in white sarsenet, with a white
veil—" was the admiration of all who beheld her, but
her modesty was her best ornament." She kept her veil
on the whole of the day. How truly French this is! [1]

Dorothy's irony, however light and harmless, is
perhaps out of place here. After all, Annette was
proud (and why not ʔ) to tell the poet that the daughter
of whom she had had the sole charge and care, that
the girl to whom he had given his name without
giving it to her mother, had had a brilliant wedding
ceremony, which effaced the memory of her irregular
birth. The mother had done her utmost, thrown
away the last of her gold to attain, as it were, this
exaltation of their daughter. What matter if she did
it according to her ideas, which were those of a
humble French bourgeoise, and in the manner of her
country! The absent father, the kind aunt herself
who had not been able to come, would have done
better here to check their sense of humour.

In the marriage certificate, it is stated that Wordsworth had given his consent by a certificate, dated

[1] Harper's William Wordsworth, II. p. 218.

17th October, 1815, registered by and left with Maître Dehérain, a notary in Paris. This certificate does not exist, but another one kept in the same office merely specifies that Caroline acted " with the consent of her father, which she declares having in her possession.[1]   Besides, as we shall see, this certificate does away with the idea that a dowry was settled by the father on his daughter, although for three years Wordsworth had really been living at ease, thanks to his sinecure as stamp distributor for Westmorland, which brought him £400 a year. It is a great pity that all trace of Annette and Caroline should have been carefully destroyed by the poet's nephew and first biographer, for we might have found elsewhere the proof that the father contributed to his child's settlement.

It would be the more desirable, as the Wordsworths knew very well how modest were the resources of mother and daughter. In her letter of 4th April, 1816, to Mrs. Clarkson, Dorothy wrote:

The young person is married to M. Beaudouin's Brother. We have just had a letter from them both, written a month after their marriage. I believe him to be a noble-minded, excellent man, and she seems to have well-grounded hopes of happiness, provided poverty can be kept out of doors, but though their present income is very well for two persons, it is not enough for a family. Mr. B. has a place under government, and will have, they assure us, a certain increase of income in a short time; besides, C.'s mother has the promise of a place for herself or one of her family in recompense for services performed by her for the royal cause, but I fear she may wait long for this, as the poor king has not

---

[1] *Cf.* Appendix III.

wherewithal to reward all who deserve it. In case of Mr. B.'s death, his widow will have half the amount of his present income as a pension.[1]

There is no longer any question here of the dowry, which had been mentioned in the letter on 31st December, 1815, without any explicit statement as to who would provide it.

The marriage contract left with Maître Dehérain seems to dispose of all ideas of a settlement by the father on the daughter. But for still another reason, it is an interesting document. It is here, more than in the brilliant ceremony of the marriage itself, that we see Annette in all her glory as a loyal royalist. Round this empty table, witnesses to this dowerless contract, sat several of the great people of the day to do homage to the poor mother of a portionless girl. The certificate is so strange, the form so exceptional, that it would deserve complete quotation: the widow of the Prince de Beauveau, the wife of the Duc de Montmorency, the Vicomte de Montmorency and the Marquis d'Avaray, both peers of France, and the Baron de Tardif, field-marshal, came thither among a dozen people to declare "they held the marriage as desirable," whereas the contract specifies that the whole fortune of the pair is their personal property, and stipulates for a total jointure of two thousand francs.

A few of the witnesses are already known to us from their connection with Annette: the Vicomte de Montmorency, Jean Marie Pardessus, the Baron de Tardif. The member for Loir-et-Cher, Josse de Beauvoir, came to greet the former Chouanne in the

---

[1] Harper's *William Wordsworth*, II. p. 172.

name of the department in which she had fought. The Marquis d'Avaray acts in a way as the delegate of the king himself; for his brother, the Comte d'Avaray, until his death in 1810 had been the most faithful companion and dearest friend of "Monsieur" (afterwards Louis XVIII.), during the emigration.

Following the example of the noble friends of the Vallons, the most famous officials of the time known to the Baudouins also came and signed their names. It constitutes, as it were, a review of the *ultras* of the Restoration. This imposing series of witnesses marks the zenith of Annette's career. It was to her what was later to Wordsworth the famous Oxford ceremony in 1839, when he was proclaimed a Doctor of Civil Law amid the cheers of the audience. An honour devoid of all solid advantage to her, we must admit—a flash of soon extinguished splendour.

Some of the persons who had taken part in that demonstration, however, realised the painful contrast between Annette's rights and her fortune. They joined a numerous body of others who had formerly been helped by her, or had been witnesses of her courageous services, to petition for a royal recompense in her favour.[1] Annette asked for that reward to be given not to herself but to her daughter, and finally a lottery office was applied for on behalf of Madame Baudouin. We again find in this petition the signatures of the Marquis d'Avaray, of Josse de Beauvoir, of the Baron de Tardif, of J. M. Pardessus, and of a score of other noble persons in addition. Among the latter, we shall only note the Marquis de Bartillat, the Duc de St. Aignan, the Comte de Salaberry. Not content with signing, J. M. Pardessus added a

[1] See Appendix IV.

marginal note to the request, stating that the claim was not for a favour but for justice. As to Salaberry, the fanatical monarchist whose perfect honesty was acknowledged by his very enemies, the former Chouan who had once plotted for the king with Annette in Loir-et-Cher, he let his indignation at the thought that nothing had been done for her find full expression. " I am more qualified than anyone," he wrote in the margin, " to testify to the complete devotion and rare disinterestedness shown by Madame William for the twenty years that I have known her, and I am sorry to bear witness to the neglect into which her rights to the king's bounty have fallen." The Baron de Tardif points out the services rendered by Annette during the Hundred Days:

The king's cause and interests having drawn me to the side of Madame William during the interregnum of the Hundred Days, I assert that there did not exist in the whole of France at that unhappy period so zealous, devoted and courageous a woman as she.

It seems that the petition did not produce all the desired effect. Three claims were successively put in, in March, June and September, 1816. In the end, Annette must have got some small help, since in 1825 she appealed for an increase of her pension, with what success we do not know. She had to work for her living in some humble situation which we cannot trace. After the dazzling days of splendour, she disappears again into obscurity.

XIX

But she is happy in having by her side her daughter and grandchildren. After the marriage we find the Baudouins living at 47 Rue Charlot, with Annette.

Her son-in-law, Jean Baptiste Martin Baudouin, then head of an office at the Mont de Piété, was to hold in that office the positions, first of inspector, then of sub-director. He was in 1816 a good-looking man of thirty-six, the second of three brothers, the two others being officers. He lived till 1854. It is pleasant to see the close friendship that united him with his brothers, especially with Eustace, the younger, who was at all times an active intermediary between the Vallons and the Wordsworths. Eustace also had for his sister-in-law, Caroline, who was of his own age, a sincere affection. " He is very much attached to his sister-in-law, and has given us a very pleasing account of her," wrote Dorothy to Mrs. Clarkson (4th April, 1816).

The very year of her marriage, on 27th December, 1816, Caroline gave birth to a first child, a daughter, by whom the English poet's French posterity was to be assured. The godfather was her grandfather: " Mr. Williams (*sic*) Wordsworth, *propriétaire*, residing at Rydalmount near Kindal, Westermorland (*sic*), the child's maternal grandfather." [1] The poet, not being present at the christening, was represented by Nicolas Bailly, now doyen of the councillors of the Cour de Cassation; the godmother was the wife of the father's elder brother, *née* Caroline von Hönigshof, a Viennese by birth. It is touching to

[1] Birth certificate of Louise Dorothée Baudouin. Paris, Mairie.

WORDSWORTH'S DAUGHTER
CAROLINE BAUDOUIN (*née* VALLON)

WILLIAM WORDSWORTH
From the picture by B. R. Haydon, *c.* 1830

find among the child's names that of the English
aunt who had always borne her a tender affection.
She was christened Louise Marie Caroline Dorothée.
She was, it is true, generally known as Louise, but
this mark of affection given to the poet's exquisite
sister pleases us. We could wish that the idea had
originated with William himself, the godfather.

The Baudouins were to have two other daughters:
Anne Léonide, born on 15th December, 1819,
who died before she was six, on 15th October,
1825, and Marie Marguerite Caroline, born on 12th
November, 1823. So the poet's daughter had already
with her two little girls, the one nearly four years, the
other nine months old, when the Wordsworths at last
paid her, in October 1820, their so long delayed visit.

Wordsworth, with his wife and sister, accompanied
also by his friend Henry Crabb Robinson, were
coming home from a tour on the Continent. We
find a few details of that visit in the diaries kept by
Dorothy, Mrs. Wordsworth and Robinson.[1]

Having arrived in Paris on 1st October, the poet
and his sister went the next morning to see the
Baudouins. It was arranged that they were all to
meet, Annette and Mrs. Wordsworth included, in
the Louvre at one o'clock. It was in the Museum,
then, that the first interview between the former
lover and the wife of the poet took place. The same
day, the Wordsworths left the hotel where they had
put up to take up their abode in the Rue Charlot,
near the Baudouins. It is Mrs. Wordsworth who
tells us so in her diary. Robinson notes down a little
more explicitly on 3rd October: " Having break-
fasted alone, I repaired to the Rue Charlot and was

[1] See Harper, II. p. 319.

introduced to Mrs. Baudouin, a mild, amiable little woman in appearance." [1] On the 7th he goes to see the Wordsworths, but finds they are out. Thence he goes and calls on Madame Valon (*sic*). On the 8th, he again calls on the Baudouins, where he learns that the Wordsworths are not yet back from Versailles. He returns once more and finds Dorothy. Always Dorothy!

The diaries also speak of Captain Eustace Baudouin's great kindness to the visitors; he was their attentive guide everywhere. No allusion is made to the poet's grandchildren. We know from another source that Wordsworth found less enjoyment at the Louvre than at the Jardin des Plantes. It is just possible that he took young Louise Dorothée to the garden to show her the animals.

This is all the record we have of that meeting, the last which took place between the Wordsworths and their French friends. A psychological novelist might find in this situation matter for a long chapter. Yet no very vivid emotions seem to have been stirred by the meeting. Time had blunted sensibilities and vanities on both sides. We may be sure that the greeting which passed between Mrs. Wordsworth and Annette was simple, friendly and devoid of bitterness. Besides, the ignorance of French on one side and of English on the other, obviated the difficulty of conversation. All passed very happily indeed. "We have had great satisfaction at Paris in seeing our Friends whom I have mentioned to you. Of this when we meet." [2] Thus wrote Dorothy to Mrs. Clarkson after her return to England.

---

[1] See Harper, II. p. 319.
[2] See Harper, II. p. 319.

XX

It may be during this visit that Wordsworth gave
Annette or Caroline his pencil portrait by Edward
Nash (the counterpart of the one he offered to
Southey in 1818). He also presented them with a
splendidly bound copy of the two-volume edition of
his poems published in 1815, a precious but un-
decipherable gift for his French descendants, who
in the first generation seem to have stubbornly kept
themselves ignorant of the language in which he had
become famous. One of the two volumes is still in
the family's possession, but the other has disappeared.

The only attempt to become acquainted with
Wordsworth's poetry seems to have been made by
the youngest daughter of Caroline. Marie Marguerite Caroline Baudouin, whose charming features
are known to us through a photograph, had become
in 1845 the wife of M. Marquet, a high official of
the prison administration. In the year which followed
her marriage she desired to know what were those
poetical works the fame of which had been propagated
in France by Pichet, Sainte-Beuve, Philarète Chasles,
Fontaney, and of which many reviews spoke with
respectful and devoted admiration. She then lived
at Melun, her husband being the prison director.
" A former professor of foreign literature " wrote
for her an account, well informed on the whole, of
the general characteristics of Wordsworth's work.
He speaks in rather pompous style of the originality
of the English poet, and highly praises his intimate
and familiar verse. He speaks judiciously of the
Lakists, and of the purity of their inspiration, both

moral and religious. He explains Wordsworth by commenting on Lamartine, for whom his admiration rises to enthusiasm. Finally he acclaims in Wordsworth the poet of childhood, and, by a skilful transition, concludes:

O benevolent and venerable poet, may France always love and keep with reverence thy beloved children—thou who hast worked so long for the moral well-being of youth, and hast entrusted to an alien soil thy dearest affections!

The booklet of nine pages was dedicated " to Madame A. Marquet, granddaughter of the illustrious poet Wordsworth." [1]

When the " former professor of foreign literature " wrote these lines, Wordsworth was still alive. Annette had been dead for five years. We read in the death register:

In the year 1841, on 10th January, died in Paris, Boulevard des Filles du Calvaire 11, in the 8th *arrondissement* Marie Anne Vallon, known as William, an *employée* [2] aged seventy-five years, born at Blois (Loir et Cher). Spinster.

Poor words, the pathetic quality of which will be felt by those who know what moving realities are here hidden under the designation of " spinster," under the " known as William," and who picture the straitened and arduous life of the seventy-five-year-old " employée."

She was buried in the Père-Lachaise cemetery. When in 1846, at the death of Caroline von Hönigshof, the wife of Colonel Baudouin of St. Firmin, the

---

[1] See Appendix V.

[2] The word probably means that she held a small state office.

Baudouin family bought a burying-ground there, Annette's remains were exhumed, and together with those of her granddaughter, Anne Léonide, transferred to the vault in which, in their turn, her son-in-law and her daughter Caroline were to be laid to rest near her. On the slab we can still read these words:

Anne Léonide Baudouin, born 15th December, 1819, died 15th October, 1825, and Marie Anne Vallon Williams (*sic*), born 22nd June, 1766, died 10th January, 1841, exhumed and laid together on 28th November, 1846.

What were Wordsworth's feelings at the news of Annette's death? Doubtless, not very profound. He was old and was outliving himself. This was the time when with circumstantial inaccuracy he dictated to Miss Fenwick senile notes on his poems, amongst others those to *Vaudracour and Julia*, which seem like an effort to bury his French love-affair in oblivion. In this year, moreover, all the remaining passion in his soul gathered itself into a kind of egotistical despair at the thought of the impending marriage of his English daughter Dora with Mr. Quillinan. From this time onward, everything else seems to have been indifferent to him. He was to die in 1850.

It deserves notice, however, that in the year after Annette's death he published a translation into English verse of a short French poem that appeared in a volume entitled *La Petite Chouannerie ou Histoire d'un Collège Breton sous l'Empire*.[1] The English translation bears the name of *The Eagle and the Dove*. Was not there some recollection of Annette's

[1] By A. F. Rio. London, Moxon, 1842.

bravery as a Chouanne in the praise given to the
" beardless boys " who boldly fought against the
soldiers of the French Emperor?[1]

After all, we can only speak with hesitation of the
old man's feelings, for all trace of the letters exchanged between the English and the French families
of the poet has been lost. Yet it is certain that the
correspondence was not closed with the visit in 1820
of which Dorothy said she had kept so pleasant
a remembrance.

After Annette's death, and Wordsworth's appointment as poet laureate (1843), the Baudouin family
made a move to obtain some recognition by him of
their claims to relationship. As soon as Wordsworth
himself was dead, Mrs. Wordsworth, the poet's
nephew, Bishop Wordsworth, and Crabb Robinson
almost decided to make some public statement
relating to the affair of 1792. The question was
very seriously discussed among them. But the
Baudouins' efforts seem not to have been insistent.[2]

A few words will suffice to bring the story to its
close. Caroline Wordsworth (Madame Baudouin) was
to outlive her father twelve years. Her life, less
eventful than Annette's, has no history, but her
features are known to us. It will be remembered
that, according to her mother and to M. Eustace
Baudouin, she strikingly resembled the poet. Looking at her portraits, all taken in her later years,
this resemblance is chiefly visible in the chin and

[1] I thank Mr. Gordon Wordsworth for pointing out to me
this poem and its probable relation to the Annette episode.

[2] I owe this information to Professor Harper, who found
the facts among the Crabb Robinson documents (diary and
letters preserved at the Dr. Williams library in London).

cheek-bones, which are rather prominent both in father and daughter. What strikes us is a look of gaiety which, in the earliest photograph, is almost a laugh, not that " convulsive inclination to laughter about the mouth," observed in Wordsworth by Hazlitt, which is already so noticeable in the drawing by W. Shuter in 1798, and which is found again in the pencil portrait by Edward Nash.   In Caroline it is a mixture of kindness, mirth and playfulness which is said to have endeared her to her friends and grandchildren.

She was buried in the same grave as her mother, and her children had these words, still legible, carved on the stone:

To the memory of our mother Anne Caroline William Wordsworth, the widow of M. Jean Baptiste Baudouin, former sub-director of the Mont de Piété, born on 6th December, 1792, died in 1862.

She died on 8th July. The certificate states that she lived on the left bank of the Seine, 3 Rue Jacob, and that she was a *rentière* (an independent lady).

The poet's posterity was assured through Caroline's eldest daughter, for Madame Marquet died childless in 1864.   Louise Marie Dorothée Baudouin was twice married, first to M. Judesretz, twenty-one years older than herself—an unequal and unhappy union. Left a childless widow in 1849, she went back to her parents, and two years later, being then thirty-four, she married Théophile Vauchelet (1802–73), an historical painter who was well known under Louis Philippe.   A pupil of Herseut and of Abel de Pujot (the latter acted as witness at his wedding), he won the Grand Prix de Rome in 1829, and first painted religious subjects, but the Versailles museum contains several historical compositions by him. He has preserved in a fine portrait the features of his mother-in-law, Wordsworth's French daughter.

Madame Vauchelet died on 2nd October, 1869, leaving two daughters who are now dead, but through whose children the poet's descent is continued, numerous and prosperous.

XXI

IN the course of this story we see two beings so strongly contrasted that only the illusion of young love could ever have drawn them together and created between them a passionate union, which, impatient of conventions and obstacles, they had once hoped to render permanent. Wordsworth and Annette were separated by language, political opinions, tastes and temperaments. Chance had brought together these two natures, far asunder as the poles, and created between them a connection which, in various forms, was to last all their life long.

What is extraordinary in their adventure, is not so much the ardent passion of its initial stages as its gradual conversion into a friendship which later takes the form of a somewhat distant family tie, a calm and vague connection which was not only accepted by the poet himself, but imposed by him upon his inner family circle. What gives to this liaison its particular aspect is the part played by the pure and kind

Dorothy, whose gentle heart sympathised from the beginning with the foreigner loved by her brother and was drawn towards their child,—Dorothy who little by little became, in the place of William, the habitual correspondent of his former mistress. Perhaps still stranger is the perfect equanimity of the legitimate wife, not ignorant of the past, but giving her sanction to it, and, without trace of retrospective jealousy, of the slightest bitterness, going to visit the woman who gave her husband his first child.

It is a singular situation. Instead of lessening our idea of Wordsworth's goodness and his conformity to moral laws, his love-adventure only shakes it a moment to strengthen it immediately afterwards. He may as a young man have strayed from law and order, but soon we know not what secret power induces him to make of what might have been but a passing folly, a sort of first marriage followed by a separation by mutual consent, without clashing or violence. He builds up a new life, a new family, quite within the law this time, without severing his ties with the old one. We can understand how the French Wordsworths could have believed, from the second generation onward, that a marriage had taken place between Annette and William during the Revolution, a marriage of which neither the place, the date nor the conditions were known, no doubt concluded after Caroline's birth, maybe illegal, that is to say performed by some non-juring priest, as was often done at the time, and as the catholicism of the Vallons rendered it probable. The documents that have been found, it must be owned, do not encourage this belief, but surely Wordsworth carried

I

even into his irregularity a constancy and gravity which consecrated it.

If, unhappily, on account of the loss of the documents which might reassure us, a painful uncertainty is left as regards the help given by him to his mistress and their child, either in 1792, in 1802, or at the time of Caroline's marriage, on the other hand we can at any rate be glad that he did not keep his past a secret. He neither condemns nor disowns it. Most of those who surround him are aware of it; first his guardians and his sister, then his wife and some of his friends had been told the story. No reserve was imposed on Dorothy, who ingenuously writes about it to Miss Pollard or Mrs. Clarkson. This sincerity is pleasing. It breathes of simplicity and nature. It is only later that mystery enveloped the whole adventure. It does not seem that Wordsworth as a man was responsible for it, except perhaps in the later years of his life.

It must, however, be acknowledged that as a poet he helped to blind the world. More intent on education than on pure truth, aspiring to play an almost sacerdotal rôle, he allowed an image of himself, more edifying than exact, to take shape in his verse. He hardly showed his weaknesses and mistakes, or if he confessed them at all, did so in terms so moderate that no one could have guessed all that was hidden by certain harmless-looking words. He did even more, since he undertook to retrace his own youth, and practised in his *Prelude*, where all is true, the deceit which consists in the omission of embarrassing facts. He himself warns us of it, in a way ; but he cannot prevent the effect of the suppressions he thought himself

entitled to make. The three books of *The Prelude* on
the Revolution do not contain the whole truth of
his stay in France nor of the feelings of the poet
during the three years which followed his return to
England. The crisis he underwent was not merely
intellectual. Politics did not wholly engross his
thoughts, nor guide all his actions. There was
Annette and there was Caroline. It is impossible
to-day to re-read these books without seeing their
shadowy faces in the background. It is impossible
not to wonder, or smile, at more than one statement,
more than one analysis of self which is warped
because they are absent from it.

There is another, an æsthetic, reason for regret.
The reality was richer, more complex and humane
than the simplification of his experiences given us
by Wordsworth. His poetry suffers from his over-
expurgation of Nature. Though this part of his
poem is powerful, how much more vivid were the
emotions he really experienced in France! Wordsworth between Annette and Beaupuy at Blois, his
walks with the heroic officer who infuses into him
his revolutionary fervour, alternating with stolen
interviews with her whom he loves and who bears
in her bosom the fruit of their passion! Or again
at Orleans when in September he exults at the
proclamation of the Republic, then falls from these
high summits of enthusiasm into the agony of
knowing Annette to be in hiding and unhappy, while
he cannot devise the means of repairing his fault
and of preventing her coming shame. In only one
of his poems did he have the frankness to hint at
the whole affair, though he shirked the opportunity
of recounting it in full—namely, in the *Descriptive*

Sketches, which he wrote during that same tumultuous year. Hampered, however, by his subject, he could only express in it his love and remorse without fusing them with the rest. He could but force into a merely picturesque poem those fits of exultation and of bitter melancholy which he felt in 1792. He casts into the past, into an excursion which, as we know, was an enchantment to him, regrets and remorse which came to him two years later. In the midst of his Alpine rambles he stops now and then, and sighs. He declares that human joy is brief and he numbers among life's scourges " the spectres of conscience." He has no hope of overcoming his despair—" Save in the land where all things are forgot." But, save in the *Sketches,* his principle was reserve, the escape from the dramatic and the stifling of passion. Hence the peculiar character of his poetry, which involves the limitation of its grasp on the imagination and consequently of the number of his readers.

The episode of Annette thus helps us to form a juster appreciation of his poetry. It is not that it becomes an essential element of it. The significant fact is that the adventure is suppressed as a thing adventitious and foreign. Yet its value is not wholly negative. We have seen that it gave the poet subject-matter or inspiration for several poems written by him before 1802—those in which he represents some forsaken wife or some girl-mother abandoned by her seducer.

Even his fine lines to Lucy and to Mary Hutchinson take a deeper meaning when we are aware of the other passion, so different, which once burnt in the young man's heart, and of the comparisons which are implied in the tribute he offers them.

This episode thus affords us a favourable point whence to survey his life, his character and his works. It leads us to a revision of our judgment. This is the best justification of these pages.

But in relating it with all the details possible in view of the rare and scattered nature of the documents, which are difficult to find and to connect with one another, we have also tried to call up, against the background of the Revolution, through which a whole family live their eventful history, the image of his French mistress; and on the whole, her weaknesses being admitted, she appeared to us worthy of a sketch—the eager and generous girl who could captivate the young poet's love, who, asking nothing for herself, with no bitter recriminations, could retain the friendship of the mature man. Indeed hers is the better part, since she gave more than she received.

Her courage as a monarchist is admirable, whatever opinion we may hold of the *chouannerie*. She who, in the service of her cause, from devotion to her political friends, many a time risked being arrested, thrown into prison and perhaps guillotined, assumes the aspect of a heroine.

She was also a devoted sister whose energetic decision once saved from wreck the brother she loved. And throughout, she splendidly performed her maternal duty to the child whom circumstances had left to her sole care, to her sole affection. She succeeded, according to her lights, in ensuring for her a purer, less troubled and penurious existence than her own. She, who was an *employée* to her last day, managed that her daughter should be a *rentière*.

And if she had a taste for worldly vanities, it is in the wedding of that daughter, Wordsworth's daughter, that she gave full scope to her inclination, in the first months of 1816 which mark the zenith of a chequered existence, half shade, half sunshine.

APPENDICES

APPENDIX I

GENEALOGY OF THE VALLONS

JOSEPH LÉONARD, known as VALLON, surgeon; b. 1660, d. 1755

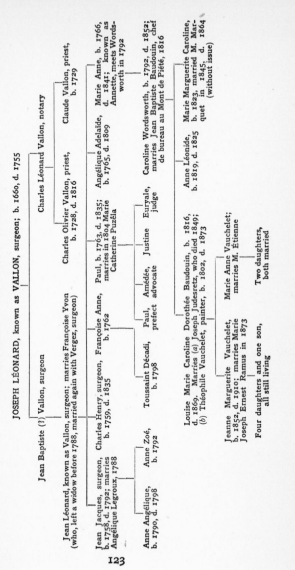

Jean Baptiste (?) Vallon, surgeon

Charles Léonard Vallon, notary

Jean Léonard, known as Vallon, surgeon; marries Françoise Yvon (who, left a widow before 1788, married again with Vergez, surgeon)

Charles Olivier Vallon, priest, b. 1728, d. 1816

Claude Vallon, priest, b. 1729

Jean Jacques, surgeon, b. 1758, d. 1792; marries Angélique Legroux, 1788

Charles Henry, surgeon, b. 1759, d. 1835

Françoise Anne, b. 1762

Paul, b. 1763, d. 1835; marries in 1804 Marie Catherine Puzéla

Angélique Adelaïde, b. 1765, d. 1809

Marie Anne, b. 1766, d. 1841; known as Annette, meets Wordsworth in 1792

Anne Angélique, b. 1790, d. 1798

Anne Zoé, b. 1792

Toussaint Décadi, b. 1798

Paul, prefect

Amédée, advocate

Justine

Euryale, judge

Caroline Wordsworth, b. 1792, d. 1852; marries Jean Baptiste Baudouin, chef de bureau au Mont de Piété, 1816

Anne Léonide, b. 1819, d. 1825

Marie Marguerite Caroline, b. 1823, married M. Marquet in 1845, d. 1864 (without issue)

Louise Marie Caroline Dorothée Baudouin, b. 1816, d. 1869. Marries (a) Joseph Judesretz, who died 1849; (b) Théophile Vauchelet, painter, b. 1802, d. 1873

Marie Anne Vauchelet; marries M. Étienne

Jeanne Marguerite Vauchelet, b. 1852, d. 1910; marries Marie Joseph Ernest Ramus in 1873

Two daughters, both married

Four daughters and one son, all still living

123

APPENDIX II

LETTERS OF ANNETTE VALLON TO WILLIAM AND DOROTHY WORDSWORTH

(20th MARCH, 1793)

[THE following letters have been recently discovered by M. Guy Trouillard in the Records of the " Département de Loir-et-Cher. Fonds du Comité de Surveillance du Département; liasse L. 2060." They now bear the mark LD 990 *bis*.

The two letters were addressed as a single one to

Monsieur Williams Wordsworth
Staple Inn No. 11
London
Angleterre.

The letter to William Wordsworth is written on both sides of a single sheet of paper. The address is framed in the latter part of the letter, the paper being simply folded in and sealed. On the broken wax of the seal a V is still discernible.

The letter to Dorothy fills up two sheets of very close handwriting, the last sentences being written in the margin. The sheets are of smaller size than the one used for the letter to William, so as to be enclosed in the latter.

The ink has faded, but the characters remain quite distinct. Some words have been obscured or torn here and there by the folding in of the flaps and the breaking of the seal. One or two more are blotted out by an ink-stain. My conjectural restorations of those words are indicated by brackets.

Annette's spelling is quite personal, irregular and arbitrary. I have tried to preserve it throughout. She

uses no punctuation, but it seemed preferable not to
follow her in this. Commas and stops have been restored
to make the letter easily intelligible.]

I

LETTER TO WILLIAM WORDSWORTH

BLOIS, le 20 mars.

Je lai enfin reçu cette lettre que j'attendois avec ten
d'empressement. Elle m'a trouvée bien affligée. Je
craignois que tu ne fus malade. Ta lettre a neuf jours
de date. Il est inconsevable comme la poste nous sert
mal. Si mes lettres pouvoit arriver à toi aussi vite que
mes pensés qui y sont continuellement je ne serois pas
toujours dans des craintes pénibles. Mon imagination
ne me donne que des inquiétudes sans jamais me donner
un instant de plaisir.

Tu doit à présent avoir reçu deux lettres que jai ecrittes
depuis la date de ta dernière. J'y répont à celle de ta
sœur. La terre n'en a pas produit deux comme elle;
elle fait lhonneur de son sexe. Je désire bien que ma
Caroline lui resemble. Que jai pleuré, mon cher Williams!
quel cœur! quelle âme! comme elle partage bien les
malleurs qui macable, mais que je suis fâchée de voir
qu'elle est tourmenté raport à nous! En grâce, mon ami,
tranquilise la, dit lui que je lui promet de m'armer de
tout le courage possible pour suporter ton absence, comme
je l'en assure moi-même; je serois plus consolée si nous
étions marié, mais aussi je regarde presque impossible
que tu t'expose [au voyage] si nous avons la guerre.
Tu serois peut être prit prisonier. Mais où m'égare mes
desires? Je parle comme si je touchois à l'instant de
mon bonheur. Ecrie-moi ce que tu pense à ce sujet et
mets la plus grande activité à hâter le bonheur de ta fille
et le mien, mais sur tout s'il n'y a pas le moindre risque,
mais je croit que la guerre ne sera pas longue. Je vouderois voir les deux nations [réconciliées]. C'est un de

mes vœux les plus sincère. Mais surtout informe [toi d'un] moyen pour nous écrire en cas que la correspondance entre les deux royaume fut interompue.

Ta sœur me parle [de notre] petit ménage avec un entousiasme qui me fait grand [plaisir]. Que nous serons heureux, ô mon tendre ami; oui [on] sera heureux. Je te le promet. Ta fille fait des progret qui m'enchante. Tâche de faire ton possible pour me la donner bien tôt pour ne plus m'en séparé, cette chère petite qui rit à présent si bien, qui connois déjà sa pauvre mère et qui bientôt demandera son père. Vien, mon ami, mon mari, recevoir les embrassemens tendre de ta femme, de ta fille. Elle est si jolie, cette pauvre petite, si jolie que la tendresse que j'ai pour elle m'en fera perdre la tête si je ne l'ai pas continuellement dans les bras. Elle te resemble de plus en plus tous les jours. Je croit te tenir dans mes bras. Son petit cœur bat souvent contre le mien; je croit sentire celui de son père; mais pourquoi, Caroline, est-tu insensible? pourquoi ton cœur ne s'agitte-t-il pas quand celui de ta mère bat tems? O mon ami, bientôt il le sera agité quand je lui direz: « Caroline, dans un mois, dans quinze, dans huit jour, tu vas voir le plus chérit des hommes, le plus tendre des hommes.» Alors le cœur de ma Caroline sera émue, elle sentira la première sensation et ce sera de tendresse pour son père. Je te prie, mon cher petit, de faire passer aussi tôt cette lettre à ma chère sœur que j'aime de toute mon âme, de l'engagé de ne rien dire à ton oncle; ce sera un combat pénible qu'elle aura à soutenire. Mais tu le juge nécessaire.

J'arrive de me promener avec ma petite, mon ange (car elle en a la candeur); elle a été fort guaie; je lui ait dit que j'allois écrire à son père. Je lai bien embrassé pour toi. Je me chagrine bien de ce qu'elle a toujours son pouce dans sa bouche. Elle vas s'abîmer les yeux; elle les tire ces yeux; et ce sérois grand domage car elle les a bien beau. Je n'en écrie pas bien long car je nai pas le tems. Je veux retourner voir la petite à six heure; il en est bientôt cinq edemie. Je tai écrit une lettre bien longue

dimanche.   J'espère recevoir de tes nouvelles bientôt.
Adieu, mon ami, dit bien à ta sœur que je vouderois bien
apprendre qu'elle est plus tranquille.   Aime toujours ta
petite fille et ton Annette qui t'embrasse mil fois sur la
bouche, sur les yeux et mon petit que j'aime toujours,
que je recomande bien à tes soins: adieu, je t'écrirez
dimanche.   Adieu, je t'aime pour la vie.

Parle-moi de la guerre, ce que tu en pense, car cela
m'ocupe beaucoup.

II

Letter to Dorothy

Blois le 20 mars 1793 mercredy à 10 heure du matin.

Si il est consolant pour moi, ma chère sœur, de voir
l'intérêt que vous prenez à [mes tris]tes chagrins, je
m'afflige bien en même tems de ce qu'ils vous rendent
si malheureuse.   Mes sentimens sont audesus de mes
expressions.   Je n'en trouverois pas qui vous renderoit
au naturel ma vive reconnaissance; elle égale l'attachement que j'ai pour ma chère sœur.   Ces deux sentiments
sont gravé dans mon âme; le tems ne fera que les aug-
menter, surtout quand une espasse imense ne nous
séparera plus, quand je pourai dire mil fois le jour à me
sœur que je l'aime avec cette tendresse que je sens déjà
bien vivement.   Que vos lettres sont touchante, que j'ai
de peine à en soutenir la lecture!   Je les arrose de larmes
comme celle de mon ami.   Votre dernière ma fait une
sensation si vive; à chaque ligne je voyois la sensibilité
de votre âme et cet intérêt si touchant que vous prenez
à mes peines.   Elle sont grande, ma chère sœur, je vous
l'avoue, mais ne les augmantez pas en vous affligant trop:
l'idée que je vous rend malheureuse est cruelle pour moi;
oui ces moi qui trouble votre repos, qui fait couler vos
larmes.   Calmez-vous, ô ma chère sœur, mon amie, j'ai
grand besoin de cette assurance pour ne pas être plus

inquiètte.   Je vouderois pouvoir vous donner quelque
consolations, mais hélas! je ne le peu; cest à moi d'en
chercher auprès de vous.   Ces dans l'assurance de votre
amitié que je trouve quelque soulagement et dans l'invio-
labilité des sentiments de mon cher Williams.   Je ne peu
être heureuse sans lui, je le désire tous les jours, mais
j'aurai assé de raisons pour me soumettre au sort qu'il
faut que je subissent.   Je l'apelle souvent à mon secour,
cette raison qui trop souvent est foible et impuisante
auprès de mes sentimens pour lui: non, ma chère amie,
jamais il ne ce fera une idée juste du besoin que j'ai de
lui pour être heureuse; maîtrisée par un sentiment qui
cause tous mes chagrins, je chérit toujours son empire et
l'influence qua sur moi [un amour?] cher à mon cœur
sous cesse ocupée de lui.   Son image me suit par tout;
souvent seule dans ma chambre avec ces lettres, je crois
qu'il va entré.   Je suis prette à me jetter dans ces bras et
lui dire: «Vient, mon ami, vien essuié des larmes qui
coule depuis longtems pour toi; vollons voir Caroline,
ton enfant, ta ressemblance; vois ta femme, le chagrin
l'a bien changée; la reconnois-tu? oui, à cette émotion
que ton cœur doit partager avec le sien.   Si ses traits sont
changé, si cette pâleur te la rend méconaissable, son cœur
est toujours le même.   Il est toujours à toi.   Reconois ton
Annette, la tendre mère de Caroline.»   Ah! ma chère
sœur, voilà l'état où je suis continuellement; revenu
de mon erreur comme d'un songe, je ne le vois point,
le père de mon enfant; il est bien loin de moi.   Ces
scène se renouvelle bien souvent et me jette dans une
mélancolie extrême.

Mais, ma chère amie, je vois sans y pensé que loing de
vous consoler, je vais encore éguilloné les chagrins que
vous avez raport à moi, mais je ne peu rien vous cacher,
ce seroit faire injure à la sœur de mon chere Williams,
la tante chérit de ma fille, de lui caché la moindre choses.
Non, je ne le ferai pas.   Ces dans le sein de l'amitié que
l'infortuné trouve des consolations; cest dans celui de
ma sœur que j'aime à mépencher, mais si vous vous

attendrissez sur mon sort, je partage bien aussi les désa-
gréments du vôtre. Vous n'avez personne à qui vous
puissiez librement confier l'état pénible de votre âme
et que vous êtes obligée d'étouffer des larmes que votre
sensibilité vous arrache. O ma chère sœur, que je suis
malheureuse de savoir que vous l'ête raport à moi;
jamais, non, jamais je ne pourai trop vous dédomager de
tout ce que vous soufré pour moi. Mon ami partage
bien ma reconnaissance; il m'avoit bien dit, ce cher ami,
qu'il avoit une sœur charmante, mais que le tableau qu'il
ma fait de votre âme est inférieur à ce que je vois dans
vos écrit! Non, mon cher Williams, tu ne m'en as pas
dit assé. Je veux un jour lui en faire reproches quand
nous serons réunit; mais quand viendra-t-il? Ah! que
je le croit encore éloignez! Il faut que je l'achette encore
par bien des soupires. Mais quand nous y serons, ô ma
sœur, que nous serons heureux! Et toi, mon ami, désire-
tu ce jour aussi ardament que ton Annette? Quand tu
sera environéz de ta sœur, ta femme, ta fille, qui ne
respirerons que pour toi, nous naurons qu'un même
sentiment, qu'un cœur, qu'une âme, et tout sera reportée
à mon cher Williams. Nos jours coulerons tranquillement.
Je jouirez enfin du calme que je ne peux sentire qu'auprès
de toi, qu'en te disant de *vive voix* que je t'aime.

Et vous, ma sœur, vous l'aimé aussi, mon ami; comme
moi vous ête privé du bonheur de le voir; que vous
êtes malheureuse si l'absence vous est aussi pénible
qu'à moi, mais vous n'êtes pas si éloignéz. Plus souvent
qu'Annette vous recevez de ces nouvelles; vous vous
envoyiez vos pensés; et moi, trop souvent les lettres que
je reçois de lui ont huit jours de dates; la dernière que
j'ai reçu était datée du 8 mars et je ne l'ai reçu que le 14;
jétois déjà bien inquiette; sa lettre m'a fait un plaisir
inexprimable, et celle de ma chère sœur me fait encore
pleuré quand je vois que mes moyiens de consolation sont
insufisant, que je ne pourois sans la trompé lui dire que
je suis heureuse. Mais je peu vous assurer que si jétois
assez heureuse pour que mon cher Williams put faire le

voyage de France pour venir me donner le titre de sa
femme, je serois consolée. Dabort ma fille auroit un père
et sa pauvre mère jouiroit du bonheur de l'avoir toujours
avec elle. Je lui donnerois moi-même des soins que je
suis jalouse qu'elle reçoivent de mains étrangère. Je ne
ferois plus rougire ma famille en l'apellant ma fille, ma
Caroline; je la prenderois avec moi et jirois à la campagne.
Il n'est pas de solitude où je ne trouvas des charmes avec
elle. Je ne peu vous dire à quel excès je porte la tendresse
pour ma fille. Quand je la tien dans mes bras, je lui répette
souvent: « Caroline, ma chère fille, tu na pas ton père;
il est bien loing de toi, pauvre petite. Si il te voyois, et
ta chère tante, combien il te trouveroit intéressante. Les
aimera-tu, mon enfant? Oui, je leur prometerai pour toi.
Apelle ton père, ma petite. Bientôt je te prenderai dans
mes bras; j'irez au devant de ce père qui a coûté tant de
larmes à ta mère; tu le serera dans tes petit bras; tes
petite lèvre lui donnerons un baizé bien tendre; elle lui
seront chère, ces caresses inocentes.» Oui, ma chère
sœur, j'irez lui porter son enfant. J'ai déjà montré à
Caroline la route; j'irez encore demain avec elle; nous
l'apellerons, mais il ne nous entendera pas; ny vous non
plus, ma bonne amie, vous n'entenderez pas, mais vous
penserez que presque tous les jours je m'échape à deux
heure après-midy pour aller avec ma fille dans les lieux
qui me sont chère puisque j'y ait été si souvent avec votre
frère. Je parle à Caroline comme si elle entendois; je
lui dit: « Regarde, ma fille; c'est ici le couvent où a été
élévée ta mère, où souvent avec ton père nous nous
sommes attendrie en pensant à ces jours heureux de
l'inocence où tu es actuellement. Conserve la longtemps,
ma Caroline, si tu veux être heureuse; sois toujours
sourde aux cris des passions; ne connois jamais d'autres
sentiments que l'amour pour ton père, ta tante et ta
mère.» Elle me donne les plus grandes espérances; je
crois qu'elle répondera aux bontés et aux soins que vous
vouderez bien prendre d'elle, car, ma chère sœur, vous
serez sa seconde mère, et je suis persuadée [du soin]

que vous metterez à travailler à en faire une seconde vous-même.

Vous voulez que je vous parle d'elle; ces bien me prendre par mon foible. Je ne tarie point en parlant de ma fille. La tendresse maternelle ne m'aveugle point, mais je suis orgeuieuse de l'entendre dire par tous ceux qui la voyient que ce n'est pas un enffant ordinaire. Le premier jour qu'elle a sorti, la femme qui la portois fut arrêttez par plusieurs personnes pour l'admirer. Elle passa par la maison, mais je ne peu vous répettez ce qu'éprouva son infortunée mère. J'en ait parlé dans ma dernière à mon ami. Ménagez ma sensibilité en me permettan de passé sur cette scène qui m'a valu une journée entière de larmes. Elle coule encore. Je m'arrette. . . .

Je reprend la plume. C'est encore de Caroline que je vais entretenir sa tante. Jobserve tous les progrets quelle fait; il son rapide. Elle est d'une vivacité qui se dévelope tous les jours. Il n'est plus possible de la faire manger couchée comme sont tous les enfants. Il faut qu'elle soit assise sur les genoux et elle s'y tien seule. Bientôt elle voudera manger seule. Le jour que j'ai reçu votre lettre et celle de Williams, je m'empressai d'aller lui dire. Je lui fit baiser les deux et après je lui mit la vôtre dans ces mains; elle la garda tout le tems qu'elle manga. Je croit, la pauvre petite, qu'elle partageois ma joie; elle rioit beaucoup. Jus de la peine à lui ôter pour lui donner celle de son père. Elle la prie avec la même vivacité, et l'une après l'autres, je lui fit mettre ses lèvres et j'y apliquois les mienne. Cette soirée délicieuse finie trop tôt et je ne pouvois la quitter; ces le seule plaisir qui me reste, de la voir; je n'en jouit jamais assé. Après midy je vais aller lui faire baisé cette lettre. Je ferai une croix dans l'endroit, et je me procurerez le plaisir de la baisé après elle. Je croit bien que ma chère sœur en aura ausi de choisir cette endroit pour y appliquer ces lèvres et recevoir les sentiments les plus tendre de la mère et de l'enfant. Mon ami qui vera cette lettre avant vous en fera autems. Ne fesons plus qu'un tous les quatre, ma

K

chère amie; un jour viendera que, réunit ensemble, notre unions sera indissoluble.

Vous avez rit de ma vanité, du soins que je met à habiller ma fille; oui, cest pour moi un grand plaisir. Cette petite toque rose qui lui vas si bien a un grand prix pour Annette. Mon cher ami la baisé. Je me rapelle lui avoir fait baisé tout ce qui devait servire à son enfant. Ce tendre père, cet ami sensible, a touché tout ce qui fait aujourdhui la parure de ma fille. La première fois qu'elle la porté, ces moi qui lui mit, moi-même après l'avoir baizé mil fois. Je lui dit: « Embrasse, ma Caroline, cette coiffure. Ton père n'est pas si heureux que moi; il ne te la vera pas; mais elle doit têtre chère; il y a mis sa bouche. »

Je le fait sortire actuellement tous les jours deux heure; elle se porte bien mais elle ma donné bien de l'inquiétude pendant quelque jours. Vous avez dû la voir dans une lettre que je vous ait écritte. Actuellement vous devez avoir reçu deux.

Avant de finire ma lettre, ma bonne amie, je vous recomande bien de ne pas vous affligée, de chacher autems que vous le pourez à votre oncle et votre tante les raisons qui comande à vos larmes de couler. Je vouderois bien pouvoir vous dire pour les arrêttez que je suis heureuse, mais je vous tromperois; vous ne pouriez le croire; mais au moin je peu vous assuré avec vérité que si il est possible que mon ami puisent venire me donner le titre glorieux de son épouse, malgret la cruelle nécessité qui l'obligera de quitter aussi tôt sa femme et son enfant, je suporterai plus aisément une absence pénible à la vérité, mais je serai à même de trouver dans sa fille un dédomagement qui m'est interdi jusqu'à cette époque.

Je suis forcé de finire mais je ne fait que commancer. Le papier finie toujours trop tôt. Je me procurerai le plaisir de vous écrire bientôt. Je volle chez ma fille aussitôt que j'aurai dîner; jemporterai ma lettre avec moi. Adieu, ma chère sœur; non, pas adieu, car je vous direz encore deux mot. . . .

Il est quatre heure. Le tems passe vite avec Caroline. Elle a bien baizé cette croix; chaqu'une nos tours, nous l'avons fait. En grâce, ma chère amie, écrivé-moi bien tôt et dite-moi que vous êtes un peu consolé; j'attens cela avec impatience. Pensé toujours à nous; je vous payie d'un parfait retour, car vous mocupée bien souvent.

Je suis ocupée à présent a faire des bas pour Caroline, car bientôt on ne poura plus la tenir dans ses langes; elle est trop vive. Je vois avec peine qu'elle naura pas les cheveux si blon que je l'espérois; il brunissent tous les jours ; jétois bien contante parce qu'il me sembloit qu'elle les aurait de la couleur de son bon père et comme les vôtres.

Je vous embrasse de tout mon cœur; je voudrais bien que vous fusiez près du tems où vous verez mon tendre ami, mon cher Williams. Que vous serez heureuse! Vous lembrasserez avant moi, mais fait le bien pour nous deux et pour Caroline.

Adieu, ma chère amie, adieu. Aimez toujours celle que vous chérit, aimez aussi [de cœ]ur votre petite fille.

APPENDIX III

MARRIAGE CERTIFICATE OF CAROLINE WORDSWORTH

(MARCH, 1816)

*Les 6 et 15 mars 1816. Devant Me. —— et son collègue
ont comparu:*

Madame Louise Étiennette d'Archiac, veuve de M.
Ferdinand Gérôme de Beauvau, prince de Craon, et
demoiselle Jeanne Marie Bonne d'Alpy, demeurant toutes
deux à Paris, rue Ste. Croix 22,

Madame Anne Louise Caroline Goyon de Matignon,
épouse d'Anne Charles François, duc de Montmorency,
demeurant à Paris, rue de l'Université,

M. Mathieu Jean Félicité, vicomte de Montmorency,
pair de France, chevalier d'honneur de son altesse
Royale Madame, gouverneur du château de Compiègne,
demeurant à Paris, rue de Lille,

M. Claude Antoine de Béziade, marquis d'Avaray,
pair de France, lieutenant général des armées du Roi,
maître de la garde-robe de sa Majesté Louis XVIII., et
Angélique Adélaïde Demailly, son épouse, demeurant
ensemble à Paris, rue de Grevelle, faubourg St. Germain
No. 85,

M. Claude, baron de Tardif, maréchal de camp, ancien
officier supérieur des gardes du corps du roi, chevalier
de Saint-Louis, demeurant à Paris, rue Jacob No. 22,

M. Auguste Guillaume Josse de Beauvoir, deputé de
Loir et Cher, demeurant à Paris, rue de Grenelle, hôtel
de Bourgogne,

M. Jean Marie Pardessus, professeur à l'École de

134

Droit, membre de la chambre de Députés, demeurant à
Paris à l'École de Droit,

M. Guillaume Antoine Baron, directeur général du
Mont de Piété, demeurant à Paris, rue des Petits Augustins
No. 20,

M. Étienne Barthélemy Dysarn de Villefort, chevalier
des ordres de Saint-Louis et de Saint-Lazare, sous-direc-
teur du Mont de Piété, rue des Vieilles Andriettes No. 4,

Madame Anne Françoise Gabrielle Pontonnier, épouse
de René Victor Pesson, inspecteur de la navigation du
bassin de la Charente Inférieure, et Louise Constance
Pesson, sa fille, demeurant à Paris, rue des Saints Pères 17,

M. Pierre François Dubonexie de Pinieux, chevalier
de l'ordre royal de St. Jean de Jérusalem, demeurant à
Paris, rue Neuve des Mathurins No. 18,

et Madame Marie Louise d'Hönigshof, épouse de M.
Baudouin de St. Firmin, lieutenant-colonel, demeurant
à Paris, rue du Cherche-Midi No. 25,

Lesquels ont déclaré qu'ils ont pour agréable le mariage
dont les conditions civiles ont été arrêtées par le contrat
dont le minute précède entre M. Jean Baptiste Martin
Baudouin et Mlle. Anne Caroline Wortsworth (sic).

The contract itself is as follows:

Par devant Me. —— *ont comparu:*

M. Jean Baptiste Baudouin, chef de bureau au Mont
de Piété, demeurant à Paris, rue de la Tixéranderie No.
82, fils majeur de Georges Baudouin, propriétaire et de
Marie Anne Étienne, son épouse, actuellement sa veuve,
demeurant à Montbard, Département de la Côte d'Or,

et Mademoiselle Anne Caroline Wortsworth, fille
majeure de M. W. Wortsworth et de Mme. Marie Anne
Vallon, dite William, demeurant la demoiselle à Paris,
rue Paradis 35, faubourg Poissonnière, M. son père à
Grasner près Kendal en Angleterre, et Mme. sa mère
à Paris, rue Charlot 47, au Marais,

Stipulant et contractant la dite demoiselle pour elle et
en son nom, du consentement de M. son père qu'elle

déclare avoir et en présence et du consentement de Mme. sa mère, d'autre part.

ARTICLE I

Les futurs époux seront communs en biens conformément aux articles du Code civil.

•   •   •   •   •   •

ARTICLE III

Les dits futurs époux déclarent que toute leur fortune est mobilière et ils mettent en communauté tout ce qui appartient à chacun d'eux, en conséquence il n'est fait aucune appréciation de leurs apports.

ARTICLE IV

Stipulation d'un préciput de deux mille francs.

Dont acte le 16 février 1816.

Ont signé :

A. C. WORDSWORTH,

M. A. VALLON *dite* WILLIAM,

BAUDOUIN.

APPENDIX IV

PETITION TO THE KING ON BEHALF OF ANNETTE VALLON

(MARCH–APRIL 1816)

Les soussignés supplient Sa Majesté de leur permettre d'attester le courage, le dévouement, la constance avec lesquels Madame Williams née Vallon a sauvé, caché et secouru dans les temps les plus orageux de la Révolution un nombre infini de François fidèles sujets du Roi, dépouillés, persécutés et poursuivis pour la cause de leur Dieu et celle de leur attachement à la dynastie des Bourbons. Ils attestent aussi les sacrifices de tous genres qu'elle n'a cessé de faire pour la cause du Roi.

Signé :

MM.

BÉRENGÈRE, DUCHESSE DE BEAUVILLIERS DE ST. AIGNAN.

LE MARQUIS D'AVARAY, lieutenant-général, maître de la garde-robe du Roi.

HYPOLYTE DELAPORTE, fils de l'intendant de Loraine et Barois.

DE BELLEFOND, chevalier de St. Louis, capitaine d'infanterie.

LE MARQUIS DE BARTILLAT, officier aux gardes du Roi.

THÉODORE DE MONTLIVAULT, officier de marine du Roi.

THÉODORE DE PÉRIGNY, commandeur de l'ordre royal et militaire de St. Louis, membre de la Chambre des Députés.

LE COMTE DE MENOU.

MALET, maréchal de camp, atteste avec plaisir le contenu.

LE COMTE DE QUINEMONT, officier des gardes.

LE MARQUIS DE COURTAVEL, maréchal de camp.

LE COMTE DE SALABERRY, membre del la Chambre des députés.

LE COMTE DE BÉRANGER, maréchal de camp.

DE LUSIGNAN atteste tous ces faits.　Ils sont à sa connaissance.

DE ROSTAING, chef d'escadron de dragons.

LE CHEVALIER DE LA ROCHEMOUHET déclare que Madame Williams lui a sauvé la vie en exposant la sienne.

LA BOISE DE RAISEUX, commandant les royalistes sous les ordres de M. Le Veneur, commissaire de sa Majesté, dans l'Orléanois.

VICOMTE DE MALARTIC, major-général de l'armée royale du Maine, atteste que Madame Williams a rendu des services signalés pendant le temps de l'insurrection de la Vendée et avec un désintéressement qui lui donne des droits aux bontés du Roi.

LE DUC DE ST. AIGNAN, PAIR DE FRANCE.

LE VICOMTE D'OSMOND, commissaire extraordinaire du Roi, atteste la vérité des faits.

　　Pour copie conforme.

　　Certifié conforme et véritable :

　　　　feme WILLIAMS VALLON

　　　　　　(*signature d'Annette*).

[en marge]

　Je suis plus à mème que personne d'attester le dévouement parfait, le désintéressement rare que Mde. William a montrés depuis vingt ans que je le connois, et malheureusement j'atteste aussi l'oubli où ses droits à la bonté du roi sont laissées.

　　CTE. DE SALABERRY, officier vendéen, député du dépt. de Loir et Cher.

[en marge]

Depuis vingt-cinq ans je connois Madame Williams
Vallon; il est impossible d'avoir porté le dévouement et
les sacrifices pour la cause royale et les malheureux plus
loin que ne l'a fait cette dame.

Elle mérite non pas *in leret* [intérêt?] mais justice et
jamais Justice n'aura été mieux rendue qu'en la récom-
pensant par un bureau de Lotterie qu'elle sollicite pour
Madame Beaudouin sa fille.

PARDESSUS,
Député de Loir et Cher.

[en dessous]

Les soussignés députés de Loir et Cher certifient à
tous ceux qu'il appartiendra que les originaux des Pièces
ci dessus énoncées sonts restées entre leurs mains.

JOSSE BEAUVOIR,

Paris, le 4 avril 1816.　　CTE. DE SALABERRY.

[2 feuille]

Madame Williams depuis vingt cinq ans n'a cessé de
donner des preuves du plus parfait royalisme. Elle a
caché, secouru, un grand nombre d'Émigrés et de prêtres
persécutés. Elle en a fait échapper des prisons et elle a
par son zèle et son courage arraché à la mort beaucoup
de sujets fidèles du Roi en exposant ses jours. Dans tous
les tems elle a servi la cause Royale avec un désintéressement absolu: Dans les derniers événements qui ont
plongé la France dans le deuil, elle a fait des traits de
courage, sans calcul personnel. Ne voyant que son attachement à la Dynastie légitime, elle affichoit la nuit
les proclamations, les répandait le jour, fesait partir les
Braves qui vouloient se dévouer pour la cause des Roi.
Elle joint la copie certifiée des témoignages nouvelles
qu'elle a obtenus.

Le cause et les intérêts du roi m'aiant rapproché
pendant les cent jours d'interrègne de Madame
Williams, j'atteste qu'il n'existait pas à cette

époque si malheureuse dans toute la France un
être aussi zélé, aussi dévoué et aussi courageux
qu'elle, et je suis heureux de grossir de mon
nom la nombreux et respectable liste qu'elle
présente,

LE BARON DE TARDIF,

Maréchal de camp et ancien officier supérieur des
gardes du corps.

Paris, le 6 mars, 1816.

APPENDIX V

TO MADAME A. MARQUET

GRANDDAUGHTER OF THE ILLUSTRIOUS POET WORDSWORTH

LITERARY NOTE ON WORDSWORTH, POET LAUREATE OF HER MAJESTY THE QUEEN OF ENGLAND

WILLIAM WORDSWORTH, distributor of stamps at —— in the county of Westmorland, is one of the most original poets living at the present time. He is the poet of real feeling. No praise is too high for his lyrical ballads, such as *Hartleap Well*, *The Banks of Wye*, *Poor Susan*, *We are Seven*, *Ruth*, the verses *To the Cuckoo*, *Margaret*, *The Complaint*, and a thousand other pieces, of marvellous beauty and perfect originality.

Wordsworth has achieved a reputation of the highest order amongst the most intelligent class of readers, not only because he can keep his poetic practice within the limits of his theory, and confine himself to the common language of men—a language which can be employed with much charm in such poems and pieces as those we have just quoted—but also because he can express his most profound thoughts in words of the greatest beauty, availing himself at the same time of the most daring poetic licence. Wordsworth is deservedly the head of the poetic school of the Lakes.

This school took its origin in the first French Revolution—or, rather, in the feelings and opinions which brought about that revolution. The poetic literature of England had degenerated, towards the end of last century, in the hands of the imitators of Pope, into all that is common and mechanical. It had need of new elements, and found them in the principles and events of the revolution which had just broken out in France. By virtue of the impulse it received from this political cataclysm it was suddenly raised from the most servile imitation to the highest degree of originality and paradox.

The change which took place in literature at this time was as complete and at the same time as startling as that which took place in politics. The minds of politicians and poets were in a state of ferment, and, according to the ideas current at the moment, the whole world was to be renewed, and to become according to nature. Everything known as authority or fashion, elegance or system, was cast aside as belonging to prejudice or pedantry. Licence became extreme, and was pushed to its furthest limits. The Deucalions who were to bring about the great promised renaissance were Southey (then poet laureate) and the two authors of the *Lyrical Ballads*, Coleridge and Wordsworth. They founded their poetic doctrine on nature alone, stripped of all art. This poetry reduced to one level all distinctions of nature and society; it shattered the golden images of poetry, and stripped them of their splendid coats of arms, so that they might be tested in the crucible of ordinary humanity. The proofs are to be found throughout the works of the poets named, and, above all, in the numerous compositions of him to whom this article is particularly devoted.

The Lake School is the school of nature; it was, at the end of the eighteenth century, what the school of imagination had been two centuries earlier. Under the great Queen Elizabeth, Imagination was the prototype of the poetry of the time, and imagination, confined within reasonable limits, may be indeed regarded as the truly inspired guide of genius. It may justly be called the elder sister and companion of Intelligence. In poetry, the two seem to unite to form a single muse. And are not poets, in all nations, the Pilgrims of Genius, the seers and the prophets? Are they not the benefactors of the world, whose duty is to sing the beneficence and power of the Creator? What soul could be so insensible as to refuse them homage and adoration? Kings of the past, they transform it into the present. Endowed with the double faculties of seer and prophet, they unfold a prospect of the future, in turn dazzling and gloomy. They are the brilliant oracles which reveal themselves to our eyes like a pillar of flame, or like a sunbeam struggling through the clouds. Who, then, would refuse to reverence the poets?

For the poet of true feeling, there are not two different worlds, the world of sense and the world of thought; he enfolds them, he unites them; for him there is but one same universe. He does not know what delights him most —the flowers unfolding at our feet in the meadow, or the stars twinkling and, as it were, coming to birth in the firmament above our heads. Wordsworth calls the one the pure reflection of the other, for to the poetic soul of Wordsworth feeling is imagination beautifying everything. Thus poets add beauty to created things, and the puissant wand of these magicians of thought is naught else but imagination or feeling.

We can therefore justly say:

> Soyez béni, ô vous tous, pèlerins du génie,
> Voyageurs qui marchez à l'immortalité
> En léguant aux humains ces chants de verité
> Dont les anges du ciel vous dictent l'harmonie!

At the end of a religious meditation, Wordsworth makes this touching and sublime prayer:

> The Poets . . .
> Oh! might my name be numbered among theirs,
> Then gladly would I end my mortal days.

And he attained the noble aim of his genius, for his prayer was heard by the muses, the ministers of divinity.

Spenser was the poet laureate of the great Queen Elizabeth, as Wordsworth is to-day of the young Queen Victoria. Spenser had also founded a school, but a school of imagination only; nothing in his doctrine was real, save language; all was fiction and allegory. His great poem the *Faery Queen*, which he composed while private secretary to the Viceroy of Ireland, is an allegorical work of the highest order.

In Wordsworth, Poetry, Philosophy and Religion are united by a bond both powerful and fruitful—the spirit of love; and when this sentiment is developed, intelligence and imagination create within themselves vast conceptions. They produce all the emotions of the sublime and beautiful; thus, in the noblest and highest feelings of man, these three sisters, Poetry, Philosophy and Religion, are one, and this marvellous unity is constantly realised in the most exquisite of all feelings, the spirit of love.

But the purpose of Wordsworth and his school was not only to please. Their purpose was to raise, to etherealise man, to make him purer, more grateful to God, more confident of His marvellous and inexhaustible goodness. Are not poets like Wordsworth our most profound theologians? Do they not bring to us the knowledge of happiness and the sublimest morality? Their pious and philosophic muse sings in hymns and odes the sacred beauty of nature and the powerful God who created it; the song of men becomes like as the song of the angels.

Another characteristic of the poetic school of Wordsworth is that, instead of choosing elevated subjects, it concerns itself almost exclusively with humble life. Thus it is a poetry not of passion nor of imagination, but of affection and the heart. A simple labourer, a humble shepherdess can be its hero or heroine. Its principal object is to sanctify and to beautify the humblest emotions of quiet lives. The home is its altar; it rarely strays beyond the circle of family life. One might say that this poetry is peculiar to England, and is, of all poetry, that which produces the most moral effects on the lowest ranks of society. It shows them that their state is capable of producing the sweetest, the purest, the most exquisite pleasures. It opens their hearts to the voice of civilisation and humanity, and these humble and obscure people no longer rebel against their life when they see that it inspires poets who paint in the purest and most touching colours their humble actions, and their attachment to their homes. They know that the most distinguished poets of their country sing in sweet and pleasing verse " the simple annals of the poor." [1]

I know no poet belonging to this school in France save M. de Lamartine. He is perhaps not exactly the bard of the country and the village, but he is at least the poet of the affections and the heart, and in this he resembles his contemporaries of the English Lake School. M. de Lamartine is, without exception, at least in our humble opinion, the most pure—the most morally pure—of all the authors now famous in this country. There is not, I believe, in all his works, one single line which he would, at his last hour, wish to see erased, neither do we believe that there could be found one thought, or one expression, capable of bringing a blush to the cheek of the most modest woman. We could wish that there were in France at present fifty Lamartines instead of one. The moral atmosphere we breathe is in need of such a purifying agent. The pure affections which are born beneath the domestic roof, and which should rise from our hearts towards the Divinity, are now lost in the whirl of passions born of politics.

Yet the first thing we should try to cultivate is the individual character of man in his home. In that is all our being, all our existence. The duties of the citizen, who is a simple unit amongst millions like him, are but secondary. The root of the trouble is, that in times of misfortune, men grow accustomed to living too much out of themselves, to identifying themselves with public questions, and to attaching their existence to them. They unfortunately forget, in the excitement of public life, that they should follow the warning of their conscience,

[1] *Elegy Written in a Country Churchyard*, written by Gray, a secondary poet of the eighteenth century.

and remain faithful to their most intimate convictions. It is to this inner life, full of purity, of joy and of useful activity, that Lamartine in France and Wordsworth in England desire to bring back humanity. We repeat; we wish with all our heart that there were in France fifty poets of the stamp of Wordsworth and Lamartine. Such poets are the true Apostles of morality.

We cannot conclude this article, which has already exceeded the limits we had intended, without remarking on one trait of the lovable character of Wordsworth—his affection for youth, his desire to be useful to it. Thus all his works dealing with children have an atmosphere of childlike freshness, of simplicity, of naïveté, and a tendency at once moral and religious; so that the little ones, as the good Vicar of Wakefield calls the children, learn unwittingly lessons of religion and philosophy in a song about a bird or a simple flower. O benevolent and venerable poet, may France ever love and keep with reverence thy cherished children—thou who hast worked so long for the moral well-being of youth, and hast entrusted to an alien soil thy dearest affections!

By A FORMER PROFESSOR OF FOREIGN LITERATURE.

MELUN, this 10th December, 1846.

PRINTED BY
THE TEMPLE PRESS AT LETCHWORTH IN GREAT BRITAIN